STONE, WOOD,
GLASS & STEEL

STONE, WOOD,

Inspirational and practical design ideas and techniques using hard landscaping materials

GLASS & STEEL

Joan Clifton

Photography by Steven Wooster

First published in 2004 by Aquamarine.

Aquamarine is an imprint of Anness Publishing Ltd
Hermes House, 88-89 Blackfriars Road, London SE1 8HA
tel. 020 7401 2077; fax 020 7633 9499
www.aquamarinebooks.com; info@anness.com

UK agent: The Manning Partnership, tel. 01225 478444;
fax 01225 478440

UK distributor: Grantham Book Services Ltd, tel. 01476
541080; fax 01476 541061

North American agent/distributor: National Book
Network, tel. 301 459 3366; fax 301 429 5746

Australian agent/distributor: Pan Macmillan Australia,
tel. 1300 135 113; fax 1300 135 103

New Zealand agent/distributor: David Bateman Ltd,
tel (09) 415 7664; fax (09) 415 8892

A CIP catalogue record for this book is available from
the British Library.

Publisher Joanna Lorenz
Editorial Director Helen Sudell
Senior Editor Sarah Ainley
Designer Louise Clements
Production Controller Lee Sargent

10 9 8 7 6 5 4 3 2 1

contents

introduction

It is absolutely correct to say that a garden is about plants and nature. It is a place to relax, a retreat from a pressured existence and a way to reconnect with the living world. However, without bones and structure, a garden is simply a shapeless collection of plants, no matter how refined, without form and without scale. Hard landscaping, effectively the bricks and mortar of the garden, provides the means by which you can make the most of available space, creating order and progression, scale and architectural integrity.

A sensitive approach to hard landscaping can completely transform your garden from a loose horticultural collection to a theatre of backdrops and scenery, vertical dimension, thrills and excitement, from which the vegetation emerges as stars and supporting cast.

This book explores the different materials currently available for outdoor construction, including natural, composite and new technology synthetics, guiding you through their individual characters and strengths. It examines the uses for which each material is most appropriate, working through structural and performance considerations, and will help you to define your aims in garden design and achieve an outdoor landscape that gives you the retreat you are looking for and is suited to the practical needs of your lifestyle.

Above: Folding fabric screens, slotted horizontally on to steel tension wiring, make an effective, movable sun screen and provide privacy from windows above.

Opposite: Intelligent use of space has been achieved in this tiny courtyard by creating a raised timber dining deck, invisibly separated by a glass screen from the relaxed seating area below. The bold, horizontal lines of the timber steps, bench and table are foiled by tall terracotta planters and the vertical slats of the armchairs.

Right: Household wooden clothes pegs, transformed here into a semi-opaque screen, show how everyday objects can play a role in garden design.

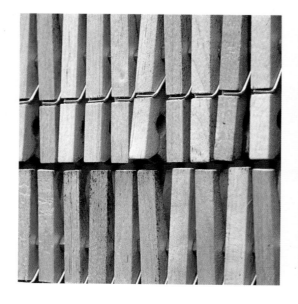

Far right: Beach pebbles, set into a wet concrete screen, make excellent decorative paving details.

Right: A substantial dry stone wall has been built of irregularly sized pieces of natural rock, which are cleverly interlocked without the need for adhesive cement.

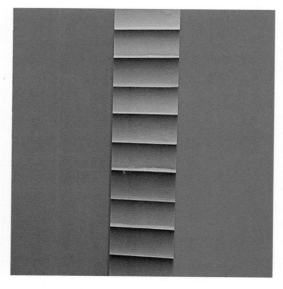

Far right: An unusual louvre detail relieves the plain surface of a painted plywood garden screen.

Right: Hand-made bricks such as these have a rustic quality that is enhanced by the use of differently coloured clays.

Far right: This raised walkway is made from slender strips of galvanized steel.

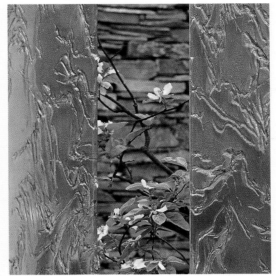

Far left: Decking made from narrow timber boards is ideal for making raised terraces or for covering uneven or unstable ground.

Left: Decorative patterns can be moulded into sheet glass to give a variety of special effects.

Far left: Bricks make ideal contrast details when used in conjunction with large paving slabs.

Left: Fragments of natural slate in different sizes are combined to make an effective ground cover detail.

Far left: Transparent glass combines wonderfully with water to make exciting sculptural features.

Left: The translucent quality of brilliantly coloured plastic film can be utilized for dramatic visual effects.

chapter one

stone

Natural stone possesses qualities that are both pleasing to the eye and gratifying to the soul. It is always at one with the landscape, conveying a sense of place, timelessness and integrity. It is a sobering thought that much of the stone we now quarry was created thousands of millions of years ago. Its strength and huge variety of colour and texture make it one of the most seductive and enduring materials to use in the garden.

Left: Smooth, pale limestone provides a clean, understated structure for this elegant formal garden. Its strong lines are reinforced by the rectangular forms of dark topiary and lawn.

stone introduction

Pushed up from the earth's core by quakes and fire, igneous rock is melted into a dense, impenetrable mass. Sedimentary stone tends to be porous and crumbly; it is made up of tiny particles deposited by floods and seawater, crushed into solid layers. These differences in the composition of stone significantly affect its performance.

The hardest and strongest stone is granite, an igneous rock containing shiny particles of mica and quartz. It is impermeable to water, resistant to pollution and able to withstand heavy traffic, and is consequently extremely heavy and hard to work, making it an expensive option. Sandstone, as a sedimentary rock, is much easier to work. Its warm, creamy tones and fine texture fit it for many uses, while its durability makes it a good long-term investment. Limestone, also sedimentary, is found in soft tones of grey or creamy biscuit, incorporating subtle veining and sometimes fossils. Luxurious marble is found all over the world. Its basic colours, which include cream/white, grey/black, amber/brown and green, are shot through with random, meandering veins of coloured minerals, giving each seam a uniquely beautiful character. Slate is an attractive and versatile material for landscape use. Welsh and Cornish slate, which is found in sombre tones of moss green, purple and charcoal, blends wonderfully with plants, trees and water, while slate from Africa and India blends the colours of hot sand and iron to enliven dynamic modern designs. Cobbles and pebbles are water-washed stones that can be used as ground cover or for decorative effect in an informal or organic design.

Stone from diverse regional landscapes ranges right through the spectrum in texture and colour. This richness makes a convincing argument for choosing natural stone over the increasing number of fake versions available, especially for use as paving. However good such copies are, they can never replicate the vibrant qualities of the real thing.

Opposite:
A contemporary version of the dry stone wall is achieved by building up thin slips of African sandstone, which "knit" together without the need for mortar. An irregular "end-on" coping, echoed by the metal fountain steps, gives the wall a dynamic finish.

Right: Rough-hewn
sandstone blocks
lend themselves
to structures for
naturalistic gardens.

Far right: Riven Indian
slate paviours exhibit
a lively combination of
colour and texture.

Right: Natural pebbles
are offset by simple
concrete paving slabs,
adding decoration to
practical flooring.

Far right: York stone is
used in this courtyard
to create flooring and
steps, and is beautifully
offset by a marble-tile
mosaic panel.

Right: Apart from its
use in paving, terrazzo
is frequently used to
make decorative items
such as planters and
garden furniture.

Far right: Irregularly
shaped flint cobbles
packed into steel
gabions make
a highly dramatic
construction device.

Far left: Riven sandstone paving slabs, with their interesting texture and soft colour, have a timeless appearance.

Left: Smooth beach pebbles filling a timber and steel mesh wall make a stylish and inexpensive screen.

Far left: Meticulously detailed stone slips make a crisply sensuous feature wall.

Left: Unevenly sized stone slips create a highly textured dry stone wall.

Far left: The small square shapes of granite setts make them eminently suitable for curving floor patterns.

Left: The hard texture and rich tones and colours of slate paving make it popular for garden floor designs.

surfaces

Real stone paving adds character and gravitas to gardens of every style. The selection of material, the way it is cut and finished, and the laying pattern will influence the final look, which can be traditional, rustic or contemporary.

Right: A sense of movement is created by this snaking limestone path, emphasized by the dark granite slips infilling the spaces between the lines.

Opposite: Terrazzo can be moulded into curving shapes. Here, a strip of pebbles emphasizes the form of the polished areas.

Below: Massive spheres of natural stone contrast with cool, smooth paving.

Stone is extremely tough and it mellows beautifully with age, improving as the years go by. A wide range of texture, colour and finish makes it possible to choose stone to suit any scheme. Paved surfaces are likely to be the largest areas of the garden over which stone is used, so it is essential to think carefully about appearance and practicality. Hard landscaping is always most effective when the material blends with, or provides an intelligent contrast to, the existing architecture of the property, so try samples *in situ* before you decide. As colour and texture may alter on contact with rainwater, run a hose over the sample stone to ensure that it will look satisfactory in both dry and wet conditions.

A common expression heard in connection with paving is "York", which has come to be applied to all sandstone paviours, though true York stone is quarried in only one region of northern England. It is strongly associated with the Georgian period in Britain, when it covered pavements and courtyards across the land; the fact that so much still exists in good condition testifies to its durability. The cost of new York stone is quite prohibitive, but reclamation dealers can usually supply old slabs, mainly salvaged from industrial sources, at a more accessible price. The only problem to watch for with reclaimed stone from such sources is that it is sometimes suffused with machine oil, so check it out before accepting delivery.

Riven sandstone slabs, which reveal the laminated structure of the sedimentary rock, are often used for traditional designs. For a more contemporary look, sawn paviours are more common; they have a clean, smooth appearance suitable for the construction of terraces, paths and steps. Unlike manufactured paving, the thickness of natural slabs can vary, so make allowance when laying to ensure a level surface.

Limestone is usually supplied as sawn slabs, perfect for clean-looking paving and steps, producing constructions of an elegant, restrained appearance. The pale colours of this stone are very fashionable at the moment, combining well with modern materials such as stainless steel and zinc, and this makes it an attractive proposition for new gardens. However, it is generally more absorbent and prone to erosion and acid damage than sandstone, so careful consideration should be given to its use in an exterior situation. Some varieties are often considered to be harder and less porous than others, but all limestone has a tendency to stain. This makes it vulnerable to marking by spilt drinks and contact with the feet of metal furniture or other objects that may rust. In brief, it is a stone for grown-ups with controlled lifestyles.

Slate has a laminated structure that enables it to be split into plates, hence its historical popularity for roofing tiles. It has great lateral strength, making it ideal for surfaces such as steps and paving. Slate paviours can be supplied riven, giving them an uneven, fragmented surface with a rustic character that is suited to naturalistic gardens. When the stone is smooth-sawn and buffed to a matt finish, it takes on a more disciplined appearance that works well over large areas and is appropriate for modern designs.

Granite is a sensible choice for paving because of its density and durability. Large slabs are costly and extremely heavy, so it may be more appropriate to use small, rectangular blocks, called setts, which are conveniently sized for making curves and detailed inset designs. The comparatively low weight of the individual blocks makes for easy handling and laying. When finished with a hammered, slip-resistant surface, granite setts are a sensible choice for slight gradients and steps. Granite can have an overly severe appearance in a domestic situation, but to help integrate the setts with the garden you can fill the spaces with a sand and soil mixture and sow grass seed instead of grouting with cement.

Terrazzo makes a highly sophisticated ground covering. Unlike the natural types of stone most commonly used as flooring, terrazzo is a manmade product that consists of marble chippings set in concrete and polished to a beautiful smoothness.

Generally thinner than paving slabs, facings are used to cover vertical surfaces such as walls and risers for steps. They are also appropriate for cladding the sides of raised formal pools and for all types of copings. While they do not play a structural role, they are used to give the appearance of solid stone to the finished structure.

Granite is a prestigious and expensive material that is frequently used for decorative facings. It is normally given a highly polished finish, revealing its dramatically fiery structure. However, this tends to give it a rather monumental appearance, so in domestic situations it is better restricted to small elements of detailing.

Polished slate can also provide a gleaming, hard appearance, but at a lower cost and of more subtle tone. Smooth-sawn facings have an understated matt finish that gives an appropriately cool, contemporary look well suited to urban courtyards and terraces. Slate offers dark and subtle shades like mossy greens

and brooding mauves and greys, contrasted starkly by the bright, crisply optimistic creamy shades of sandstone and limestone.

The highly polished finish usually given to marble leads to the assumption that it is durable. The reverse, however, is true, as it is formed from absorbent limestone and can be very unstable outdoors. It is prone to weathering by rain, sun and frost, and will stain easily from contact with acids and rust. It is therefore best suited to protected situations, such as under a veranda, or to parts of the world with a temperate climate.

Because of its fragility, marble is perhaps best restricted to small areas of detailing, such as a contrasting path border, a surround for a formal fountain or a wall decoration. Pieces of various sizes, suitable for creating neutral-toned mosaics, are sold just for this purpose and look marvellous as inset relief, teamed with a floor of pale limestone or as a contrast to dark slate paving.

Left: A crisp, formal terrace with low plinths and retaining walls is created with pale pink sandstone facings, set off by dark box hedging and toning cream roses.

Right: This formal pool is made deliberately shallow to show off the unusual, rectangular slabs of sawn slate used to construct both the liner and surround. Loosely informal planting, framed by a screen wall of the same material, makes a delicate foil to the clean, architectural lines of the design.

construction

Hard landscaping in stone provides the bones of the garden by establishing the lines of a formal composition to support the planting. It introduces focus and contrast by creating three-dimensional elements and structural features.

Solid stone construction is an expensive option but it gives the garden a wonderful feeling of solidity and presence. It is at its most effective when used in bold sweeps in a wide terrace, a dramatic wall or screen, or in a gliding procession of steps.

The textural qualities of natural stone are demonstrated most effectively when combinations of rough-hewn blocks are used, perhaps to construct a decorative wall, such as the beautifully detailed screen shown opposite. The differently sized blocks of warm-toned sandstone lock together like the pieces of a jigsaw, without mortar or cement, presenting a very modern version of the dry stone wall. By contrast, a more rustic approach can be achieved with rough-hewn slabs being used to build structures, such as retaining walls for plant borders or water features, such as a pool or fountain.

The finished look of stone facings is much more smooth and controlled than stone blocks or slabs, which would befit construction in a contemporary garden design. Facings are a more economical choice for stone usage, although the cost of the base structural work, which may be of concrete blockwork or poured cement, must also be taken into account. Stone facings are very effective so long as they are well detailed and the work is carefully executed; it has to be emphasized that the construction of hard landscaping is costly, and it is almost always best left to the professional stonemason.

Above: The wide, shallow limestone steps set the mood and scale of this formal, uncluttered terrace; the large size of the paving adds to the effect.

Right: A formal sweep of well-proportioned stone steps adds grandeur and pace to this large garden.

Opposite: Fine materials and carefully thought-out detailing characterize this elegant screen wall. Constructed from vertical columns of dressed sandstone slips linked by smooth-sawn slabs, its pale, warm colours contrast delicately with the planting of fresh green grasses and deep purple iris.

Terraces and steps extend the garden visually and provide interesting three-dimensional contrasts that are especially useful in town courtyards. Scale is a very important matter when designing a garden, and steps are perhaps one of the most challenging features to get right. They can add immeasurably to the "presence" of the garden, imbuing it with a feeling of dignity, even in a smallish space. They should be as generously wide as possible, in keeping with surrounding features, and must feel safe and inviting to walk on. A steep flight of shallow steps would be a challenge to climb and could seem vertiginously threatening to descend. So follow the basic rule: the greater the difference in height between the upper and lower levels, the longer and more gradual the flight of steps should be. Calculate for a smooth descent by designing the steps so that

Above: Sawn slabs of dark slate have been built up at different levels to create this formal pool, over which a very shallow spill of water falls. The smooth buffed finish enhances light reflection, and the colour of the stone deepens attractively when wet.

each tread can be reached comfortably in a single stride, and remember to allow a generously sized landing for arrival at the top and bottom.

When there are changes of level in the garden, structural retaining walls are required to hold back the earth contained in the resulting terraces. Because of the weight and instability of the soil, these walls need to be stoutly constructed on generous foundations, and provision must be made for rainwater to drain away freely. Retaining walls should be integrated into the design of the garden and may be multi-functional: if they can be constructed at a suitable height, they can double up as benches for informal seating or be transformed into spaces for entertaining, like the innovative bar shown in the picture below, which effectively increases the use of the courtyard without compromising its scale.

Stone water features, such as pools and fountains, add to the garden ambience, introducing sound, movement, light and energy. Bold, crisply cut slate lends itself to creating understated, contemporary structures that allow water to spill quietly over its smoothly finished surface. While slate combines wonderfully with water, its neutral tones are equally suited to restrained paving, steps and copings.

Granite's tough, enduring qualities and robust character make it an excellent choice for steps and retaining walls, though its high cost is likely to render large-scale use prohibitively expensive. Where a real dramatic presence is required, its distinctive colour and texture can be introduced as one bold statement in the form of a substantial slab. Made into a dramatic bench, granite would make a striking contemporary statement that is both decorative and functional.

Below: Changes of level create visual interest as well as diversifying the usable space in a garden. Here, a low retaining wall faced with vertical slabs of slate permits an attractive backdrop of high-level planting. A curved bar of solid stone has been added to create an innovative entertaining area, paved with matching square paviours.

sculptural effect

The textural qualities of stone can be exploited in numerous ways. It can be hewn into massive rocks or split into piercing spikes, carved into sensuously curving abstract forms or smoothed into spheres and obelisks.

Above: A curved aperture transforms a simple limestone block into a dramatic sculptural seat.

Right: A revolving sandstone sphere makes a bold centrepiece for this formal pool.

Opposite: Slim slate pillars make a striking vertical statement in this garden, contrasting well with the massive boulders beyond.

Limestone and sandstone, being smooth in texture and easy to carve, are both popular media for ornamental use. Figurative and abstract sculptural forms are normally placed as single statements in the garden, to provide a sensual contrast among surrounding plants. Tall geometric limestone and sandstone shapes, such as obelisks and pyramids, can play a more architectural role when placed formally to define an opening or focus a sightline.

A group of spheres of differing sizes can be very effectively arranged to make a Zen-inspired statement, while bold hunks of hewn slate and granite have a massive quality that brings a dynamic element to an oriental garden, suggesting powerful earth forces. The effect works best when stones are placed in groups of uneven number, balancing differently sized pieces together. On a bed of raked gravel, the overall appearance can be cool and severe, but it can be softened by adding clumps of turf or moss and small specimen conifers.

Granite is extensively used to make interesting stand-alone water features that can now be bought ready-made. The water is forced up through holes drilled through variously shaped spheres and "millstones" to create a pleasing bubbling effect. This kind of small fountain can be easily set up with a pump and reservoir to make a naturalistic feature.

Slate breaks naturally into craggy forms with immense character. It makes excellent dynamic statements but is perhaps most frequently associated with water in creating naturalistic cascades. To be convincing, these must be integrated carefully into the landscape, positioned on a naturally sloping site, and will need a powerful pumped system to push up the water. Bear in mind that large pieces of stone are extremely heavy and need expert handling.

aggregates

Small particles of any type of rock are collectively known as aggregate. Aggregates may be composed of sharp chips, or stones that have been weather-washed or artificially tumbled to produce a smooth surface.

Right: This informal curving pathway demonstrates how loose-laid slate fragments can be used to fill awkward or unusual shapes: the snaking mound of fresh green planting shows well in relief.

Below: Pebbles and cobbles of all sizes make an excellent ground cover beside beach-style water features.

Inexpensive and easy to handle, aggregates are mainly used to cover large areas, such as driveways or parking spaces. They are very useful in areas such as small courtyards, where restricted access would make paving too complicated to install. They also make excellent paths in country gardens, where architectural formality can look out of place.

For large areas such as driveways, smooth shingle and river gravel are both economical solutions. Though the yellow-brown tones of gravel are not the easiest to incorporate into a garden design, the low cost is a compelling factor and it is widely available.

Smooth, sea-washed beach pebbles are a more attractive choice, with lovely colours ranging through soft pinks, greys and mauves. They blend naturally into most landscapes, and are essential for Japanese and seashore themes. Grades from 10–15mm (½–⅝in) are about the maximum for walking on comfortably, while large cobbles and boulders make terrific landscaping features in their own right.

All loose materials move about, making them laborious to walk on, and they need regular raking to maintain an even surface. They also provide an ideal nursery bed for weeds, so it is advisable to spread a layer of hoggin, or fine gravel, and compact it firmly before covering with a thick layer of aggregate. Water thoroughly afterwards to bind the materials. A weed-suppressing membrane can be used instead, but loose stones tend to slide about on the slippery surface, making walking insecure. It is, however, essential if you are making a dry gravel garden, in which case holes can be cut to allow for planting.

A bed of contrasting coloured chippings in geometric patterns makes an interesting highlight in a courtyard. This is a purely decorative, non-traffic feature that is the modern equivalent of formal

bedding. Granite, limestone and slate offer tones of cream, grey, mauve and green; white and black marble can be used to create highly stylized effects. Polished river pebbles lend themselves to detailed mosaic to create a centrepiece in a paved area or fluid organic patterns running through a pathway. They can be sourced in neutral colours such as black, grey and white to create very sophisticated designs. These are a permanent feature able to take foot traffic, so they should be set into a wet concrete screed.

Crushed slate, a by-product of quarrying, is useful for surfacing paths and makes a decorative mulch for beds and containers, where its soft heather tones suit most plants. It is perfect for Japanese-style "dry" gardens, where its subtle colouring and low surface energy can be successfully highlighted with dynamic, asymmetric groups of bold hewn rocks. A "dry riverbed", a meandering ribbon of slate flakes arranged like naturally flowing water, makes an elegant alternative to a real stream. A sloping site is best, with the illusion emphasized by groups of larger rocks placed at intervals. These "streams" are especially effective after rain, when the wet slate comes to life with a lovely gleam.

Above: Fine gravel, or pea shingle, makes an inexpensive and neutral ground cover for large areas. Here it plays the role of "white space", against which a formal planting scheme is clearly revealed.

chapter two

wood

The relationship of timber with garden
construction is the most natural imaginable, as
wooden structures have an innate affinity with
plants. Wood is a warm, lively material, pleasing
to the touch and the eye, and offers a wide
variety of natural colour, tone and texture. It is
easy to work with, and equally suitable for bold,
strong structures such as pergolas and finely
detailed work such as furniture and trellis.

Left: Blurring the boundary between dry land and wet space,
imaginative timber viewing decks appear to float like lily pads
on this excitingly luxuriant pool.

wood introduction

Timbers fall into two broad groups. Slow-growing hardwoods derive from deciduous species such as oak and chestnut, as well as exotics such as teak and iroko. The beauty and variety of their grain and colour is unsurpassed, making them the discerning choice when budget is not a consideration. Recycled timbers, usually recovered from old factories and ships, are more accessibly priced and increasingly available. Hardwoods are effectively maintenance-free, needing no special finish or protection from the elements. They are densely textured and immensely strong, so are suitable for all garden buildings, pergolas, decking, furniture and containers.

Softwoods come from fast-growing conifers, such as pine and cedar. They are inexpensive and widely used for sheds, fences, trellis and low-end decking. To avoid the possibility of warping, this porous wood must be specified "outdoor quality" and fully protected from rot with an appropriate preservative. Planed or sanded timber can be supplied with a pressure-injected "tanalized" preservative treatment, which gives it a faint greenish tint. All edges cut later for construction must be brushed with preservative to avoid water penetration. Softwoods are not particularly attractive, but tinted preservatives enhance the natural grain and help to integrate structures into an overall colour scheme. Subtle stains are good for large areas such as fences and decking, but where solid colour is required, flat-finish outdoor paints can transform garden sheds or benches. Traditional gloss oil paints are best restricted to finer pieces of furniture.

Opposite: The fine horizontal slats of this simple wooden sculpture contrast well with the bold, vertical garden fence posts beyond.

Robust assembly methods and materials specified for outdoor use are essential for all constructions outside. Supporting posts and pillars for arbours, arches, fences and decking must be set in proper concrete foundations over a ballast soakaway, and timber should never be allowed to remain in direct contact with moist soil.

Right: Expensive but beautiful, curved planks of richly coloured, exotic hardwood make up the concentric circles of a dynamic deck.

Far right: The interesting grain revealed in these blocks makes hardwood a very attractive material for flooring applications.

Right: The exposed and softened grain of reclaimed timber can make a refreshing contrast to new wood.

Far right: Precisely cut planks with evenly spaced, countersunk screws give a clean, crisp impression against the smooth limestone paviours.

Right: Split and stripped chestnut palings secured by twisted wire make a rustic fence for an informal garden.

Far right: Brilliantly coloured paint gives an instant lift to roughly sawn planks for this screened seating niche.

Far left: These stacked rustic twigs are formed into a naturalistic dividing screen.

Left: A coating of deep-toned varnish preserves the timber and brings out the grain of rough-sawn softwood.

Far left: Smooth-planed redwood, used here for a garden shelter and seating, has a calming effect in a corner of the garden.

Left: Heavy sections of planed hardwood make excellent building blocks for retaining walls and raised planting beds.

Far left: Marine ply, varnished to emphasize its warm tones, is carefully cut and fixed to make clean, modern lines.

Left: Large sections of split bamboo are used to create a bold Japanese-style fence.

decking

The dictates of fashion now impose on the gardening scene as much as on the catwalk. It may seem that a layer of decking is covering the planet, but decking does provide an ideal solution to some common garden problems.

The huge popularity of decking is understandable from the point of view of versatility and ease of construction, but it is important to use it only where it is also aesthetically appropriate.

Where weight is a consideration, such as on a roof terrace, decking makes a lightweight surface, and when outdoor space is at a premium, it can be an ideal way to create a raised seating or dining area. A cantilevered deck, supported by pillars and guarded by a rail, can create a sun terrace with steps to a garden below. At ground level, the resulting "roof" would provide shelter for a children's play area or a hideaway for garden equipment.

A sloping site is a great challenge, but where different levels are required, decking provides a more economical solution than stone paving, walls and steps. Boardwalks generate a naturalistic feeling that associates particularly well with water and wild planting schemes. Shallow wooden steps connecting the levels will create a series of easily accessible terraced planting beds, secured by rustic retaining walls of posts or recycled railway sleepers (ties). The visual effect may be enhanced with swaying grasses to emphasize the sense of space and movement.

If softwood is to be used, it must be of top quality. Compare cross-sections of different samples, and choose wood with fine, close grain, indicating slow-grown trees from well-managed plantations.

The main downside of decking is that wet wood makes a good home for algae and can become slippery. Regular brushing with a stiff broom or cleaning with a power washer will help to remedy this, and, as an additional precaution, surfaces may be covered securely with wire mesh. Grooved planks do not really aid grip, and their appearance can be distinctly inferior to a smooth finish.

Above: A boardwalk gives access to this bold pontoon built over a naturalistic pond.

Right: A raised edging provides a smart finish for a boardwalk.

Opposite: Decking is an ideal solution for dealing with changes of level in small spaces.

boundaries and screens

Fences and screens give definition to a garden, and if made from wood they form a backdrop to the design like flats for a stage set. The style, colour and texture can be varied, though they should support rather than dominate.

Below: This unusual louvre arrangement makes a semi-opaque screen, providing an effective backdrop for planting and giving privacy to the house, while admitting daylight through the angled slats.

Enclosures may be needed to give privacy from neighbours, hide an unwanted view or, in the case of a roof terrace, provide shelter from cold winds and excessive sunshine. The cheapest option is the traditional garden fence made from wooden panels. These are available, conveniently ready for erection, in a variety of grades. The most basic panels consist of overlapping rough-sawn softwood slats, which provide a serviceable, low-budget solution. Painting or staining them in a deep, muted shade such as grey or lichen green – both of which make a good backdrop for planting – distinctly improves their rustic appearance and often unpleasant colour.

More stylish, heavy-duty alternatives can be sourced from specialist suppliers. These have the advantages of better-quality timber and design; they have a sanded finish and are pressure-treated with preservative. Various style options include a choice of slat format, top rail profile and post finials. Special features, such as keyhole openings and trellis sections, also make them useful for partial screening and garden division.

Composite wooden materials come into their own for instant garden makeovers and fun effects, especially when carefully detailed. Marine ply is a versatile medium for executing unusual designs, and even chipboard can be used, provided it is adequately sealed with an appropriate varnish or outdoor-quality oil-based paint.

Heavy, square-cut timber posts can be used to make dramatic, sculptural screening to delineate separate areas within the garden, emphasize a pathway or define a change of level. For a more rustic effect, whole tree trunks make an interesting alternative, casting ever-changing shadows across the garden throughout the year.

Opposite: This elegant screen is constructed from bold sections of treated, exterior-quality softwood.

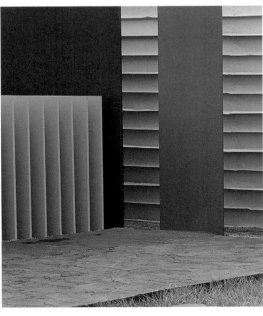

Above: Steps leading
to a dynamic moon
window screen make a
compelling invitation.
Yacht varnish, used
to seal the chipboard
(an unusual, though
economical, choice
for the garden) also
reveals its texture.

Left: This dramatic
painted screen wall is
made from sections of
marine ply with insets
of fins and louvres.

trelliswork

Latticework trellis provides a versatile aid, both ornamental and functional, for creating openwork screens and decorative finishes for walls and fences. It can be used alone for its architectural value or as a support for climbing plants.

Trellis will instantly lift the appearance of an ugly wall or fence, give added height to a boundary without obstructing light or a view, screen a working area or create divisions between different parts of the garden. Made from slim timber battens arranged in a square or diagonal pattern, it is widely available in a range of sizes and is a useful tool in any new or established scheme. It provides excellent support for climbing plants, but when set against solid surfaces it should be fixed on battens to allow air to circulate freely in the space behind. Include strong hinges at the bottom to enable the trellis and planting to be "folded" back for periodic maintenance of the wall.

Obelisks and columns with latticework infill make good architectural objects for sculptural and three-dimensional effect. They can be placed on their own as vertical statements to act as focal points in a design or incorporated at intervals along a screen wall to introduce additional height and depth.

Off-the-peg trellis panels, including *trompe l'oeil* effects to give a sense of false perspective, are particularly useful in an enclosed courtyard to introduce a feeling of space and direction. When combined with mirror to reflect light and other parts of the garden, they can create a fascinating illusion of further "rooms" beyond the real garden.

Extremely sophisticated effects can be achieved by commissioning a specialist trellis fabricator to create a design specifically tailored to the dimensions and special needs of your garden. Though this is initially costly, the outlay may prove an excellent investment for an open roof terrace or small courtyard that is entirely dependent upon its boundaries for overall background effect. Of course, if you have the necessary skill, it can be agreeable and cost-effective to construct your own scheme.

Left: This willow obelisk can be used as an architectural feature in its own right or placed in a pot so that a climber can be trained up it.

Opposite: This courtyard garden in the city benefits from bespoke trelliswork made from thin timber battens. It allows light into the courtyard but provides a degree of privacy to the garden owners.

pergolas and arbours

A wooden pergola provides an overhead "ceiling" for an outdoor area, while an arbour creates a secluded, romantic alcove. Both will contribute to the garden's ambience and will add enormously to the pleasure of your garden.

Its ready availability and ease of working make timber an excellent material for building structures within the garden. Its organic origin makes it an especially sympathetic choice when the primary purpose is the support of climbing plants.

A pergola of wooden slats, supported on strong timber pillars, can easily be constructed over an existing terrace to create an atmospheric dining or seating area that is both shaded from sun and screened from overlooking windows. Extra privacy can be gained by interweaving a translucent fabric canopy through the slats, and the timbers will also take fixings for suspended lighting for use in the evening. More conventionally, a timber pergola can be trained with flowering and fruiting vines, to give shade, colour and perfume during the summer.

The pergola is a useful device for linking or delineating areas within the garden. When it is used in conjunction with a screen wall, a strong feeling of enclosure can be achieved, creating a change of atmosphere between it and the space beyond.

A freestanding arbour can make a dramatic architectural statement for a large garden. Clothed in roses or other fragrant climbers, a large arbour makes a perfect, romantic dining area for summer days. On a smaller scale, a seating arbour makes a good feature for a courtyard: a wooden bench enclosed around the sides and top by a framework of trellis panels, it doubles as an effective plant support.

Left: This wide, vine-covered pergola provides much welcome shade and seclusion for this city rooftop garden.

Opposite: This pergola of western red cedar connects the walkway with the dining platform. Stainless steel battens support a glass canopy.

furniture and containers

Hardwood furniture always looks comfortable out of doors, and its durability makes it a sensible long-term choice. Pared-down designs have introduced new silhouettes, bringing wooden furniture right into the 21st century.

Right: Chunky sections of planed hardwood make a sophisticated alternative to railway sleepers (ties) when constructing raised planting beds.

Below: Massive planks of planed timber make a dramatic and unusual dining table.

Though good-quality hardwood products require a generous budget, they will last a lifetime and improve in looks with every year. Traditional bulky furniture, best suited to large gardens, has dominated the marketplace for a very long time, but now slimmer, contemporary designs, often with inventive folding options for easy storage, are making well-designed wooden pieces available for even the tiniest terrace.

Oak and tropical timbers, such as teak and iroko, need no special maintenance, their colour naturally weathers to a soft, silvery grey. But if this is not desirable, an annual application of wood oil or special waterproofing solution will preserve and deepen the original tones of the wood.

Tables and chairs made from softwoods may seem a cheap alternative, but when the unstable character of the wood is taken into account, together with the fact that furniture needs to be repainted annually to keep out moisture and stay looking attractive, it may not turn out to be such a good buy.

Rigorous attention to quality and design detail can make good garden furniture very pricey, but don't be tempted to use "garden-style" indoor furniture outside. Neither the timber nor the construction methods will withstand weathering.

The classic, square wooden container or *caisse Versailles* – named after the famous, demountable orange tree boxes used in the palace gardens outside Paris – is the "must have" choice for planting specimen topiary in a traditional garden. It is now taking on more contemporary lines, taller and slimmer with a tapered profile, making it a desirable choice for modern gardens. Hardwood examples can be prohibitively expensive, but softwood boxes must be preserved, painted and provided with zinc or resin waterproof liners before planting.

Right: The smooth curves of this modern teak furniture demonstrate a pared-down fluidity – a distant cry from bulky traditional hardwood furniture designs.

Below left: The profile of this sensuous oak bench makes it a sculptural statement rather than merely something to sit on.

Below right: Massive blocks of solid oak make a dramatic seating feature.

roof terraces

Wood is used to great effect in the construction and dressing of roof terraces. Hardwoods and softwoods can be worked into traditional and contemporary designs to create unique rooftop spaces that fulfil a range of practical needs.

Above: Solid timber screens pierced with panels of openwork trellis serve to separate a hot-weather shower from the terrace seating area beyond.

All roof terraces need to be sheltered from the wind and sun, both of which they will receive in large quantities. Latticed timberwork makes an ideal form of protective screening, being light in weight and versatile in application.

A screen that is intended to give protection from wind should never be solid, as this results in the air being pushed up and over the barrier, thus creating an unpleasant cold down-draught. It should instead filter the wind, allowing it to pass through gently. This is just as important for the protection of plants as it is for your own comfort, and on a roof terrace the wind is always likely to be much stronger than at ground level. The rooftop view can also be a consideration, and the screen should not totally obscure it.

An arrangement of narrow vertical or horizontal wooden slats with small spaces between them provides an elegant and effective solution. The terrace shown here demonstrates the use of wooden screening in an extremely clean, modern design that provides privacy without obscuring the view, while disguising the unsightly urban architecture at close quarters. The use of broad expanses of horizontal lines creates a clear, open effect that serves to extend the impression of space. Wind is filtered to give protection, while interesting lighting effects are achieved at night. During the day, the interplay of sunlight and shadow makes ever-changing kinetic patterns across the walls and floor.

Using wider slats and changing the spacing would alter the balance of light and shade, while a diagonal or square pattern of criss-crossed battens would entirely change the style of the terrace. Having a busier appearance, such an arrangement would make the space feel smaller, and this could be desirable if the aim is to achieve a feeling of intimacy.

Wooden screening provides essential protection for planting, which would otherwise be vulnerable to the effects of weather. It allows for the possibility of dense layers of atmospheric foliage, which would in turn create its own microclimate. Roof terraces are especially vulnerable to the forces of weather. Besides wind force, there may also be freezing temperatures, driving rain, hail and snow, and sun.

With any raised terrace, it is especially important to pay attention to sound construction methods and fixings, and to ensure that the materials used are totally suitable for their application. If wood is being used to construct guard rails and fences, the timbers must be secure and strong enough to prevent accidents, and they must be regularly checked and well maintained to prevent degeneration.

Below: The bold use of timber slats screens a roof terrace from sunlight, wind and prying eyes; by night, low-voltage lighting produces a softly glowing backdrop.

chapter three

concrete

Concrete provides an attractive and economical solution in many situations, but it is probably the most misunderstood material of all time. Its bad reputation is the result of poorly conceived public projects in the 1960s and 1970s, but many renowned designers have chosen concrete to create elegant buildings and sophisticated engineering projects, and it is now being used for imaginative interior and garden features.

Left: Concrete can be moulded into blocks or poured *in situ*, enabling the construction of complex shapes and forms such as this elegantly understated, formal contemporary pool.

Though generally associated with paving and groundworks, concrete is a perfect material for the creation of walls, freestanding screens, pools and water features. It has terrific sculptural potential and can be moulded into any shape, making it especially suitable for curved forms, which would be prohibitively expensive to carve from stone. Themed garden designs incorporating snaking walls, curved steps, round pools, undulating water slides and sinuous benches are all possible when using concrete, while some very exciting off-the-peg designs are now beginning to appear, including chairs and tables, fountains, bowls and tree planters.

Though concrete is normally grey it is possible to achieve a much brighter and cleaner-looking effect by using white cement and pale aggregate. Special pigments are also available to tint the mixture, giving the possibility of permanent colour finishes, ranging from hot Mexican pinks to soft blues and greens for a cooler, northern style. Additionally, the polished and waxed finishes now becoming fashionable for interior use can be used outdoors to bring a glamorous lift to floors, walls, screens and furniture. Because it can be moulded, concrete is defined as a "plastic" material. It is created from a mixture of Portland cement and aggregate, usually fine sand with some coarser gravel or stones. Water is then added, which reacts with the cement to harden the mix. The proportion of the mix is crucial and varies according to purpose, so take advice when ordering the materials. Basically, too much water or too little sand will weaken the mixture, while too much cement causes shrinkage and cracks.

Complex or highly detailed designs need to be pre-cast by a specialist fabricator and then delivered to the site, where special lifting and moving gear is needed. The component pieces are then assembled and fixed permanently with a wet cement mix.

Opposite: Concrete is a uniquely flexible construction material that can be moulded or assembled into any shape. Here, a bold screen features as a backdrop for the palm tree, enabling special lighting effects to be achieved. The main boundary wall, curving round behind the planting, is created from smooth rendered concrete blocks.

Right: Concrete can
be moulded into paving
blocks resembling
natural materials –
in this case, rough
timber boards.

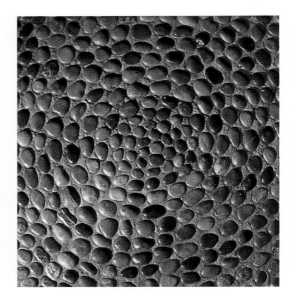

Far right: To make this
circular design, the
pebbles were set in
wet concrete.

Right: Rectangular
concrete blocks,
created in timber
moulds, are set like
stepping stones in
a gravel pathway.

Far right: Polished
concrete surfaces give
a clean contemporary
look, and lend stability
to terrace furniture.

Right: These pre-cast
concrete paviours have
been made in natural
stone moulds to
resemble York stone.

Far right: Smooth
moulded concrete
has been used here to
make a curvaceous
base for a seat.

Far left: A moulded concrete shelf is set into a rendered blockwork wall.

Left: Construction blocks, with natural bricks inserted for contrast, are used in their natural state to create a cheap and imaginative screen.

Far left: This finely detailed screen wall combines softly tinted concrete with moulded glass panels.

Left: When painted, rendered concrete blockwork provides an attractive, quick and inexpensive means of wall construction.

Far left: Good-quality, plain concrete paviours make clean and understated contemporary flooring.

Left: This screen wall is constructed from rendered blockwork; the stone sill gives the opening a distinctive finish.

walls and screens

The simplicity of concrete construction enables pure forms such as screens, walls and backdrops to be created readily on site. Colour, texture and special finishes can be included to achieve a wonderful variety of special effects.

Opposite: This spectacular lighting feature is created quite simply on a textured concrete screen wall set into a polished floor of the same material.

Below: Hand-polished concrete is a sophisticated finish for both walls and floors. Here, a pebble mosaic panel provides a decorative focus.

Walls and screens serve a number of functional and decorative purposes in garden hard landscaping. Freestanding walls may form a solid boundary to the site, providing privacy, security and a clean backdrop to the overall design. Retaining walls hold back soil in raised planting beds and terraced levels. Screens are an immensely useful device for breaking up space and can be used in differing heights and proportions to create illusions of distance and perspective. They can conceal or reveal entrances, perhaps pierced with holes to allow glimpses of a secret garden or a surprising feature, inviting entry to the space beyond. Screen walls may also act as a landscape gallery to support inlaid "pictures" formed from mosaics of ceramic tiles, glass or natural stones.

The smooth finish that can be created with concrete is one of its main advantages when working with contemporary exteriors. Its neutrality and simplicity provide a clean backdrop to the garden design and can give a real sense of scale and presence. Numerous dramatic effects can be set against it, most notably using lighting to enhance a special feature. Cascading water, with its force and energy, really comes to life at night when lit, becoming an evocative focal point, while a plain wall throws up the changing shadows and silhouettes of architectural planting and allows sculptural forms to be shown off distinctly.

There are two ways in which concrete can be used to make a wall. The simplest, needing only basic skills, is to create the structure from pre-cast concrete blocks, which are set into a foundation of wet cement and fixed together with cement mortar. This method is suitable for retaining walls and freestanding screens. An application of cement render is coated over the top, and this may be smoothed to give a clean finish, or scratched over with a brush or nails for a textured effect. Colour tint can be included in the render mix or the finished wall can be painted when dry.

A concrete wall may also be poured into place. In this case, the wet mixture is supplied to the site ready mixed and is pumped into a mould or framework known as shuttering. Decorative effects can be achieved by making the shuttering from textured materials, such as rough-sawn timber planks, which leave an impression of their grain on the surface of the concrete after removal. Where a very smooth finish is required, plywood or sheet metal will achieve the desired effect. Colour tints or decorative aggregates can be added to the mix to alter the finished effect. *In situ* concrete construction is an exacting science and it requires specialist skill to achieve a perfect finish.

flooring

Poured concrete quickly creates all kinds of flooring, including paths, terraces and steps. If necessary, shapes and dimensions can be amended easily on site, without the need for extensive planning and pre-ordering of materials.

Below: This smoothly curved concrete path "glides" elegantly, in contrast with the rough-hewn, low stone planter and the stone gabion boundary wall.

This is the simplest do-it-yourself use for concrete. After preparing the area with a bed of compacted hardcore, you need to make a simple framework from ply or softwood and pour in the wet mix. A small concrete mixer, which can be bought or hired, will ensure an even supply of material and save hours of work. Release any trapped air bubbles by tamping down with a timber batten, then smooth over with a wooden float, ensuring that there is a slight fall to the finished surface to allow rainwater to run off. Concrete has a tendency to expand and contract with changing weather conditions, so it is advisable to set a large area in sections, leaving a gap or "expansion joint" of around $^1/_8$in/3mm between each one.

A large expanse of plain concrete can look grim and industrial, but you can make the finish more interesting by inscribing designs into the surface before the mixture has set. Use a stiff brush, rake or sharp stick to create a pattern of lines, squares and circles, or even bare feet along a path.

An interesting organic appearance can be achieved with material such as leaves and stems. Leave them to set in the mixture, allowing their imprint to be revealed after decomposition. For a durable textured finish, aggregates such as pebbles or chippings may be added to the mix and exposed by gently brushing or hosing the surface just before the concrete sets. Alternatively, creative effects can be achieved by scattering material such as glass beads, shells or metal washers over the still-moist surface.

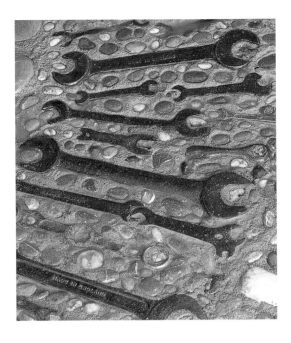

Right: Exciting effects can be achieved by setting objects into wet concrete. Here, old spanners have been combined with coloured pebbles to make an innovative, eye-catching path at minimum expense.

pre-cast paving

Pre-cast concrete paving is available in an assortment of styles and types.
It offers a range of design possibilities and the opportunity to create modern
or traditional flooring at a fraction of the cost of natural stone paving.

Below left: Concrete paviours formed in natural stone moulds, such as these made to resemble riven York slabs, are very convincing and much cheaper than the real thing.

Below right: Curving paths are easily made from loose materials. Here, concrete slabs are laid in gravel to accommodate the increased spacing on the longer side.

When taking into account the high cost of natural stone, pre-cast concrete paviours are a tempting option, especially for large areas of garden. Though historically these had a poor reputation and downmarket appearance, the production techniques have altered enormously and some very sophisticated products are now being created.

The current speciality for pre-cast concrete paving is very convincing replicas. An ever-increasing choice of slabs are available that are moulded from pieces of natural stone, thus showing a realistic relief of the original surface. Respectable replica York stone, granite, terracotta and slate are all on offer in the form of pre-cast paving. The authentic colours and natural-looking finishes are extremely convincing, especially when a sympathetic laying pattern is used. Where a simple, understated effect is desired, it is possible to obtain excellent, smooth-

textured slabs in tones varying from creamy white through taupe to deeper grey/black tones that work perfectly well with contemporary garden design schemes.

It can be a plus or a minus, depending on your point of view, but concrete paviours will not weather down, so choose your colours carefully, preferably checking the effect when both wet and dry. Cheap products have only a surface coating of colour, which can easily chip, revealing the plain grey cement inside. To avoid this problem, you willl need to choose from among the more expensive options which use quality pigments that are consistent throughout the slab. If in doubt, ask to have a slab broken to check before purchasing.

As when choosing any hard landscaping materials, it is best to select a colour and texture that blends with the surrounding architecture. Subtle tones such

as pale buff "sandstone" or greyish "slate" will blend well into the background of most gardens, while warm "terracotta" would work well on any sunny Mediterranean-style terrace. York stone replicas work well in traditional garden designs, while fake granite setts can be introduced into both modern and classical gardens.

A simple laying pattern always works best with pre-cast paving; busy designs can look confusing and tend to make areas look small and congested, while clean straight lines extend the eye to give a feeling of distance and space. Contemporary-style square tiles require a formal layout on a square grid or diamond format. However, extensive paved areas can benefit from detail strips or borders in a neutral contrasting colour, such as black or cream, to bring interest and relief. Irregular-shaped slabs, in a shade based on natural stone, tend to look best, and more natural, when set informally in a staggered pattern.

Left: Smooth and simple, these white concrete paviours are the perfect foil for the organically styled Japanese planting.

Below: Clean architectural lines determine this formal planting scheme. To add a sense of dynamism, the square concrete slabs are laid in a diagonal pattern, contrasting with the clipped cubes of topiary underplanting the trees.

furniture and ornament

Contemporary designers are increasingly embracing concrete as an exciting medium for outdoor furniture. Its mouldability and enduring qualities mean that it is brilliantly suited to sexy curving forms and gorgeous textures.

Below: Concrete's strength and "plasticity" enables the manufacture of dramatic modern pieces like this boldly sculptural furniture.

Rotting and oxidization are two of the major hazards designers confront when creating objects such as furniture and containers for exterior use. Many materials that have conventionally been used for garden artefacts, such as softwood timber and steel, need to be sealed and protected in various ways against the effects of weather, but concrete suffers neither of these problems. Provided it is correctly mixed, it rests inert and stable after manufacture and will not break down over time. It can be moulded into the most complicated shapes, facilitating designs from the pure and simple to the wild and fantastical. The colour of the material can be changed by adding pigments to the mix, and the texture can be altered at will by the addition of different aggregates. The finished surface can be rough or smooth, or even polished like gleaming silk.

Concrete is heavy, so it is an appropriate choice for freestanding objects to be used in windy situations, such as open terraces and roof gardens – though in the latter case, calculations should be done first by an engineer to check the loading. For objects placed in front gardens and public spaces, concrete's weight is also a serious disincentive to thieves.

It is an obvious choice for tabletops, especially when combined with steel or bold timber legs to balance out its weight. A small café table of this construction would withstand gusts of wind on a roof terrace. Large-scale tables and benches made from concrete embedded with a surface of crushed marble terrazzo are available; these have a pleasingly simple contemporary design, but their weight is prodigious, so they work best in a permanent position.

Many new designers are developing concrete's "plastic" qualities to produce inventive forms such as the sinuous seat shown opposite. The heavy, snaking framework sets a dynamic and sensual line that is complemented both in scale and weight by the curved wooden seat to create a stunning sculptural feature that is also an inviting place to sit.

Concrete planting containers that are a far cry from municipal street furniture are now becoming more and more available. Lovely curved bowls and tall, oversized long toms are among the most popular designs, while rectangular forms for window boxes and troughs are equally sought after.

Above: An understated
plinth is inexpensively
formed from moulded
concrete.

Right: A fabulous
example of
contemporary
furniture design,
this sensual bench
combines a sinuous
framework of moulded
polished concrete with
a curved timber seat.

chapter four

glass

Glass is a vibrant and life-enhancing material that can be glitteringly clear or mysteriously translucent, admitting light but retaining privacy. Its colours may be jewel bright or softly subtle, and its surface can be etched or screen-printed for a multitude of special effects. Created by fusing minerals and sand at fantastically high temperatures in a molten state, it can be produced in flat sheets or three-dimensional shapes by moulding or blowing.

Left: Freestanding etched glass screens in this courtyard provide sympathetic separation from the space beyond, ensuring a visually clean backdrop for the graphic planting design.

Glass has been used for centuries to create a visual link between house and garden, but technology now makes it possible to create totally clear walls and doors from vast expanses of strengthened glass, allowing a seamless connection with the garden and integrating the house with its surroundings. The traditional multi-paned conservatory has been superseded by the clear-walled garden room, which "floats" outside to create a comfortable, light-filled living space surrounded by plants and trees.

Glass is finding more and more architectural uses outside. Where protection from wind is required, panels of transparent glass give full weather protection without any loss of view. Coloured screens introduce vibrancy, while mirrored finishes coolly reflect light and extend visual space in shady or confined areas. But far from being purely functional, glass is increasingly called upon to perform extravagant decorative roles. Its ephemeral and reflective qualities are valued in creating imaginative sculptural effects, especially in conjunction with water.

Glass is a fragile and potentially dangerous material, so special care should be exercised when specifying it for use in the garden. It is vital to pay attention to the suitability and security of any fixings, and large or thick sections need professional installation. Window or float glass – made by floating the molten material on a bath of liquid tin, after which it cools into a perfectly smooth plane – is made in a range of thicknesses. Toughened (tempered) glass is very strong and breaks into tiny harmless pieces, but it must be made to size as it cannot be cut. Laminated glass, the strongest of all, is likely to be the most suitable for outdoor use: a layer of transparent plastic sandwiched between two sheets of glass holds all the pieces together if it is broken. Advice should always be taken on the appropriate form and thickness to use.

Opposite: Mirror glass can be used for numerous exciting effects in garden design. These screens arranged in an open landscape create sculptural and textural statements by reflecting light and repeated images of the surroundings.

Right: This imaginative plant cover has been created from panels of laminated glass.

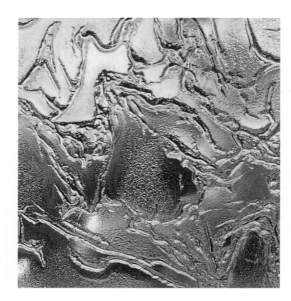

Far right: Float glass can be moulded to achieve a variety of relief designs in the surface, which can be used to echo a theme in the garden.

Right: Coloured glass can be used for numerous decorative and sculptural effects.

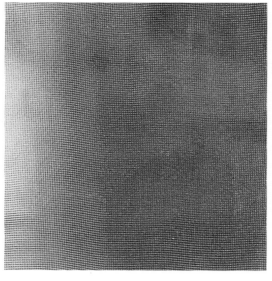

Far right: Square sheets of glass float chequerboard style on a weed-smothered decorative pond.

Right: Gently flowing lines moulded into float glass can be used to suggest movement in a translucent screen.

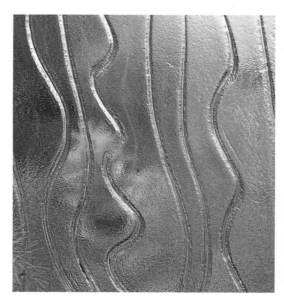

Far right: A spiral of crushed windscreen glass makes an interesting covering and adds texture to the garden floor.

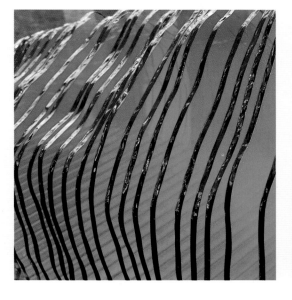

Far left: The play of light on glass makes it an especially versatile material for sculptural effect in the garden.

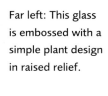

Left: Glass is used very creatively here to construct a delicate overhead canopy.

Far left: This glass is embossed with a simple plant design in raised relief.

Left: Recycled glass chippings make an unusual and exciting decorative mulch.

Far left: Hand-painted fabric has been sandwiched between sheets of clear glass to form this screen.

Left: Dangling, blown-glass droplets hang from a dramatic, sculptural "tree".

surfaces

Glass can make an unexpectedly exciting contribution to ground cover
in modern garden design, with streams of luminous glass chippings flowing
around the planting to give theatrical effects of colour, light and texture.

Right: The fashion for
mosaic planting, here
using clipped box balls,
calls for imaginative
contrasting mulches,
like these brilliant blue
glass chippings.

Below: Fantasy and
reality mix at garden
design festivals, where
this chequerboard of
glass squares floats
between gloomy
pondweed to create a
startling water feature.

Glass chippings have become very modish as a
landscaping material and can be most effective
in limited applications. This recycled aggregate is
available in numerous colours and size grades.
For practical purposes, it is best used over more
manageable areas of the garden.

For dramatic effect, chippings make an excellent,
stylized ground cover, working well as a colour
contrast for contemporary evergreen mosaic planting.
Small areas, such as around planted tubs, work
well too; both applications benefit from the use of
a water-permeable membrane to separate the
glass from the soil. Although often suggested as a
general decorative mulch, this use is not highly
recommended for reasons of maintenance: it is next
to impossible to remove fallen leaves, and soil has a
tendency to work its way up amongst
the pieces. Wherever chippings are
used, it should be possible to run a hose
through to clean them. Tumbled
chippings do have their sharp edges
removed, but caution should always be
exercised when handling them.

Glass aggregate looks really good
when underlit at night. Spread it thickly
over sealed laminated glass lighting
panels, which can be incorporated into
a geometric layout of paving and mono
planting. Chippings are also effective
when combined with water features,
especially when used with lighting.

Opposite: A fantastical, organically
designed garden demonstrates the
textural use of recycled glass in place
of paving and ground cover planting.

walls and boundaries

The existence of strengthened glass now makes it possible to create entire transparent walls around the garden so creating an invisible safety barrier or wind screen on a high-level terrace without spoiling the view.

Below: Clear plate-glass panels provide security and protection from wind without obstructing the view from this terrace.

The use of glass outdoors is a glamorous and ambitious concept, and its value is now increasingly appreciated in modern apartment developments, where every bit of space is valuable and every view desirable. Glass boundaries are now almost obligatory for luxury urban roof terraces, especially when overlooking a river or spectacular architectural panorama. The transparency benefits of glass are twofold: as well as giving access to views, it allows light in, making it useful for small or shaded spaces, where it creates an immediate impression of space and light.

Glass is an excellent solution for high-level situations, where protection from wind is required, as the heavy transparent panels give total shelter without any consequent loss of vision. However, it should be borne in mind that an invisible wall could prove to be hazardous to people and animals entering the space. In this case, an abstract pattern or a relief of stems or leaves could be etched on to the glass surface, serving both as decoration and a subtle security alert. Totally opaque sandblasted sections can be incorporated where some privacy from neighbours is desirable.

Toughened glass makes an excellent safety barricade around a roof terrace, still allowing the scenery to be enjoyed in full. Courtyards often have raised levels incorporated, which are usually protected by a timber or steel balustrade rail. A clear glass wall that creates no sense of visual barrier would be a much more desirable safety device.

Cost is an inevitable factor when working with toughened glass, and the cost and complication of installation is a significant factor when using the material outdoors. It is therefore likely to be most accessible, in budgetary terms, when used over relatively small areas, or where the value of its physical contribution far outweighs its price.

Glass blocks have long been used to build interior walls, and they provide an equally effective device for enclosures and divisions outdoors. The thickness of the blocks makes them very strong, which means

they can form part or the entirety of a substantial solid wall. Clear transparent blocks transmit the most light, though rippled and frosted finishes provide an extra degree of privacy. Coloured versions, in pale blue and green, are available for specific applications, especially a pool area, where they make an ideal shower or dressing screen. Their somewhat retro appearance will not suit every garden, however, so they should be used only in simple modernistic schemes. Ensure that the blocks are suitable for outdoor use before you buy them. It is also advisable to have them installed by a specialist.

Glass blocks make interesting punctuation in a solid concrete wall, admitting light and making a contribution as a design feature in their own right. Peephole windows will admit light and reduce a feeling of claustrophobia in a walled garden. Rectangular, round or ovoid in shape, they can be formed from fixed panes of transparent glass to break up a blank space while providing an interesting view beyond. Where this would be inappropriate, perhaps in close proximity to neighbours, the choice of sandblasted glass would retain privacy without compromising on light levels.

Above left: The visual weight of this boundary wall is relieved by the panels of translucent glass bricks.

Above: A glass brick wall offers shelter without losing light. The staggered edge gradually opens up the view to the garden.

screens

Glass has huge creative potential in its molten state, and there are
an increasing number of exciting modern artists who are responding
to its fluidity and are able to devise spectacular commissions.

Opposite: An opening between panels of embossed glass gives a tempting glimpse of the garden beyond, while the fine tracery of the design provides a visual link with the flowering tree.

A multi-coloured glass panel introduced into a plain screen wall can create a sensational effect, especially if it is positioned to take the best advantage of sunlight passing through. The changing effects of light and colour on the surrounding space add a particularly vibrant dimension to both the architecture and the planting around the wall.

Freestanding screens are often used in garden design to break up space, and they have a strong sculptural and architectural potential. Translucent or opaque coloured glass has a dramatic impact when formed into panels focusing on combinations of colour and shape for its effect. The screens can be

used singly as a feature in a courtyard or in banner-like groups to introduce a walkway, letting sunlight pass through like a version of a Mondrian painting.

Glass treated with special finishes or effects permits very sophisticated decorative elements. One of the most exciting new possibilities is screen-printing images directly on to the surface of the glass. The results can be subtle and abstract, perhaps using out-of-focus shots of leaves and landscape, or dramatically eye-catching, with a blown-up flower detail or a piece of sculpture. Such pieces work best as tall screens in a clear space, where sunlight can bring out the images to their best advantage.

Right: This textured screen makes a delicate sculptural statement in a romantic garden.

Far right: Use of colour backdrops can sometimes turn quite ordinary glass panels into something quite extraordinary.

sculptural effect

Glass and water make an excellent combination when creating modelled designs. Both are transparent and capable of reflecting light, and glass provides an almost invisible surface over which water can tumble and flow.

Right: Glass combines wonderfully with water in all manner of special features. Parts of this unique design give the illusion that the water is moving upwards.

Opposite: In this adventurous lake sculpture, statuesque screens of softly tinted glass appear to glide like tall sails past fragmented icebergs.

Below: The textural combination of glass shards and fragments of rock makes this illuminated cascade especially exciting.

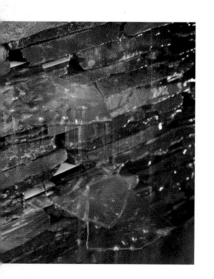

Exhibition gardens now show a staggering variety of highly technical combinations of glass and water, many of which are beyond the reach of most garden owners. But one popular and easily accessible stand-alone feature is made from small plates of sheet glass sandwiched together to form wavy columns, down which water streams and splashes. To give an extra dynamic of light and movement to these tower-like fountains, the edges of the glass are unevenly cut or moulded with a deckle finish. Magical night-time effects for glass sculptures can be achieved by up-lighting through the water reservoir.

The still, watery background of a pond provides a cool and ephemeral setting for glass sculpture. Both figurative and abstract forms are appropriate, and these are most effective when assembled from a series of individual profiles cut from coloured glass sheet. Spaced at staggered but close intervals, the glass transmits sunlight and the form appears to change in shape and effect, according to the angle from which it is viewed.

Glass is perhaps at its most exciting when forms are individually created by mouth blowing. This is a dangerous and exacting art that takes skill and courage to master. One special artist now takes nature as inspiration for pieces of glass sculpture intended to be placed in the landscape. Water droplets, stems and seed pods are reincarnated as dynamic glass forms. These works most famously include a tree of mature size dripping crystal droplets from its branches, and dazzling flower heads bursting from slender, transparent stems.

mirror

Reflections play an important dynamic role in the garden, but they need not always be provided by water. Mirror creates delightful surprises in a garden and can transform a space of any size with magical images and illusion.

Right: This impressive mirrored wall creates the illusion of a much larger garden space.

Below: A creative and amusing use of mirror as *trompe l'oeil*: a plain house wall is totally transformed by unexpected reflections of the garden.

Reflected images can cause surprise and shock, introduce light and space or create illusionary sculptural effects. Tall, vertical panels of mirror glass work brilliantly in staggered groups, especially in an area planted with a single type of plant, such as tall, slender grasses to sway in the breeze. Placed horizontally, mirrors can form an illusionary bridge reflecting the sky. When mirrors are placed to reflect each other, the combination of reflected light and repeated images suggests a limitless kaleidoscopic landscape and offers numerous possibilities of interpretation in both large and small gardens.

Where space is restricted, in an enclosed courtyard or a narrow passage, strategically placed mirrors can double the perceived space by reflecting the area opposite. It is possible to play tricks like glazing a false door in a boundary wall, thus suggesting a landscape beyond that is merely the planting in its reflection.

By reflecting light, a mirror can brighten a dingy, and otherwise unusable part of the garden. When used in conjunction with a fountain, it could completely enliven a dark, formal courtyard, multiplying the glinting effects of moving water among a planting of cool green ferns.

Always use mirror glass that has been specifically manufactured for exterior use, as you will find that the reflective backing of an interior mirror will peel off very quickly with weathering. Mirror is very heavy, so pay particular attention to fixing; for safety, always screw the glass securely to a backing of marine ply, which is then bolted to a sound wall, or set the glass in concrete foundations in the ground.

Opposite: Mirror can provoke a reaction of surprise or disbelief. A raised "boardwalk" of panels dissects staccato grass plantings with reflections of the sky.

light

Combine the sparkle and reflectiveness of glass with electric light, and a magical night-time atmosphere can be achieved, creating brilliant effects and unexpected silhouettes against the backdrop of the dark, mysterious garden.

Above: Up-lighters in the pond and against strategically placed rocks lead the eye to the coloured light boxes in the distant rocks.

Right: Projecting light on to this glass box filled with white sea pebbles makes a highly textural night-time decorative effect.

It is easy to imagine how useful floor lighting can be in a formal terrace situation as a security feature but, just as importantly, it can act as a source of subtle light-wash effects. Conventional up-lighters set in sealed glass discs in paving are quite commonplace but with imagination, and a skilled installer, it is possible to extend the concept more radically.

Large panels of laminated glass, underlit with low-voltage lamps, can turn a whole terrace floor into a huge, magical light source. By contrast, long narrow strips would create a dramatic light border around the edge of a terrace. Set into the paving, this kind of lighting provides both decorative and practical safety roles in a classically modern scheme, and could be further extended to provide glamorous illuminated steps and wall inset features.

Light boxes can be installed all over the garden to make special effects. They can be incorporated into walls, to look like night windows, or set in the ground surrounded by planting. A huge light screen made from opaque glass could serve as a dramatic backdrop for a sculpture, showing it in silhouette at night, or could simply be used alone as a bold contemporary statement in its own right. Small clear glass boxes look effective when filled with shells or washed river pebbles, while coloured glass would glow with its own kaleidoscopic effects.

Safety must always be the first consideration when working with electricity out of doors, so always have all fittings installed and checked by a professional.

Opposite: Modern technology begs the imagination to take advantage. In this luxurious town garden, glass boxes containing lighting strips are set into decking to create subtle illumination and a marvellously intimate ambience at night.

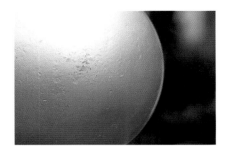

chapter five

metals

Metals are vibrant and elegant, with tremendous strength belied by light visual weight, making them among the most varied and versatile materials available. In flat sheet form, they are suitable for planters and surfaces, while metal rods and bars can be twisted into composite structures, such as gates and pergolas. Metals vary in strength, weight, texture and colour according to their mineral content, and this dictates what can be produced with them.

Left: This lively garden is partitioned by huge, double-faced, steel mesh screens filled with cobbles. Amusing squares of deep blue plastic – their shape reflected in the bold timber seating cubes – relieve what could otherwise be a brutal effect.

metals introduction

Metals have played important decorative and functional roles in the exterior environment for centuries. During the medieval period, delicate rods of black wrought iron formed intricate gates and grilles. These often incorporated the natural forms of plants and flowers, and these timeless designs continue to inspire traditional ironwork for garden decoration today. Steel, which is a highly refined form of iron, has now largely taken the place of traditional wrought iron. It is stronger and heavier, though more demanding to work by hand, and needs greater protection against rust.

Developments in production are continually evolving new ways of working with metals, resulting in exciting contemporary applications, particularly in sculpture. The flexibility of metal is the key, permitting the execution of designs as diverse as titanium-clad buildings with the appearance of burnished silk, monumental sculptures of "designed-to-be-rusty" Cor-ten steel, or towering, shimmering, stainless steel fountains.

Metals require specialist manufacturing and fixing techniques, often necessitating a high degree of hand working. This makes commissioned structures expensive, though ready-made gates, railings and planters of acceptably simple styles are available. The main disadvantage of iron and steel is their tendency to rust. Although expensive, stainless steel, an alloy steel with chromium and nickel added, is thoroughly durable and rust-free. It is becoming increasingly popular in modern exterior designs, particularly for railings and canopies, sculpture and water features.

Unless rust is a feature of the desired finish, normal iron and steel must be fully protected from moisture with coats of metal primer and special metal paint, which should be checked annually and made good to avoid rust taking hold. Steel can be galvanized by hot zinc before purchase, providing an enduring protection.

Opposite: The light-capturing quality of stainless steel suits itself perfectly to sculptural water features. The rippled flow of moisture over this smooth surface agreeably "muddles" the reflected images of the garden, while at night the backlit "moon" glows mysteriously.

Right: A decorative
embossed effect adds
texture to stainless
steel sheet.

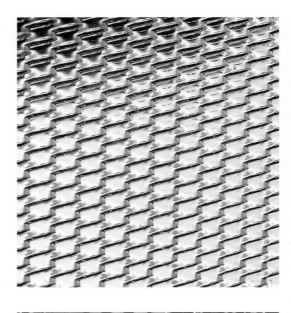

Far right: Pink
light projected over
a textured steel
screen produces
an eerie effect.

Right: Laser-cut blades
of rusty steel form part
of an organic sculpture.

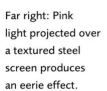

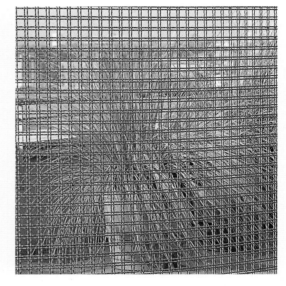

Far right: Steel
reinforcing mesh
can be used for
inexpensive,
textural screening.

Right: This wildly
organic wall is made
from crumpled chicken
netting and steel wire.

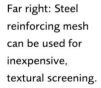

Far right: A spherical
metal finial makes a
good textural contrast
with a timber post.

Far left: Molten iron can be cast into very intricate patterns, as seen in this fabulous piece of sculpture.

Left: Cor-ten steel weathers into wonderful tones of red, brown and gold.

Far left: Simple wire mesh screens do not obstruct the view from this rooftop railing.

Left: Steel grilles make excellent free-draining, slip-resistant treatments for paths and walkways.

Far left: Perforated steel mesh is a good choice for semi-opaque screens.

Left: A beaten copper collector guides drainage water from a "rain chain".

gates, railings and screens

Most gardens are enclosed by boundaries that form an integral part of the property's security arrangements. Gates and railings made from metal can provide a secure barrier without blocking the view into or out of the garden.

Gates and railings are a traditional method of enclosing space and preventing entry. As individual pieces, metal railings are very strong, but in order to give them structural support, they are frequently incorporated with brickwork or stonework in the form of low walls, piers and gateposts.

Wrought iron, the original artist's metal, has been heated and hammered by blacksmiths for centuries into elaborate railings and gates. Its malleability, strength and visual lightness make it an obvious choice for intricately curving designs, often based on leaf and stem forms, which sit so well among plants and trees in the natural environment.

Steel, which is a highly refined form of iron, has now largely taken its place. It is stronger and heavier, though more demanding to work and needing protection against rust. A material of great character and robustness, it is heated in a forge then twisted into shape, the various sections being welded together by hand. In the hands of an artist/craftsman, it can be made into staggeringly dramatic designs reflecting both period and contemporary tastes. This is, of course, highly skilled and demanding work, which is consequently very expensive to commission. However, many ready-made designs, though much simpler in appearance, are widely available from specialist suppliers and are very well priced.

Stainless steel is playing a greater role in modern garden design with every new season. Television makeover programmes may seem to be largely responsible, but the trend is really a development from the increasing tendency to use this material for objects and fittings inside the house. It is, however, a very expensive material that needs specialist fabrication and installation.

Stainless steel is available in sheet form. It can be used flat or formed into undulating curves for both decorative and functional purposes, and is especially appropriate for dramatic reflective screens and walls. The material would be visually overwhelming as an unrelieved mass, but the effect can be lightened by cutting out shapes and profiles by laser. These might be bold geometric forms, such as combinations of rectangular slots, or softer shapes – a slender willow leaf, for example, would provide a link with the landscape, as well as being an excellent foil for what

Below: This boldly textured stainless steel gate contrasts effectively with the smooth surface and eccentric lines of the concrete boundary wall.

Above: A steel louvre screen partially obscures one area of terrace from the other, while allowing some light to penetrate.

Left: Extensive, and unusual, use of copper cladding on this apartment development gives the buildings a warm, mature look that sits comfortably alongside timber decking and balcony screens.

can otherwise seem a rather aggressive material. Sheets of perforated stainless steel, die-cut with squares or circles to form a range of grids and grilles, can be obtained from specialist suppliers. This material has an industrial feel combined with an attractive visual lightness, which can be surprisingly effective in a modern garden design. It is excellent for making semi-transparent screens and fences, especially when it is used in conjunction with raised pathways or steps in a similar material. It could work well as screening against wind on a roof terrace, though in a sunny situation reflected sunlight and heat would be intense and would need to be reduced by a filter of planting, such as bamboo.

Multi-stranded steel wire ropes are now almost obligatory on sleek, contemporary roof terraces. They combine incredible strength with low visual impact, making them an excellent device for use in safety screens and balustrades. For total security, the wires must be fixed under tension between posts, set at a

suitably short distance apart. Hardwood handrails provide solidity and framework with an appropriately nautical feel, especially in a river or coastal location.

Tensioned wires make excellent climbing plant supports that are strong enough to carry the weight of vegetation without compromising its appearance. Fix them horizontally at regular intervals on a wall or fence, allowing a small space behind for tendrils to take hold. Alternatively, make a freestanding screen with a framework of timber battens between which the wires can be stretched in a similar fashion.

Opposite: Freestanding screens make excellent punctuation marks in a design, creating textural contrasts and backdrops to planting.

Above: Courageous design and imaginative detailing can achieve impressive results in a fairly small space. Here, fabulous torches transform a contemporary garden into a theatre of light and energy at night; the shimmering steel enclosing walls increase the intensity of the effect.

Left: A curving screen of steel mesh successfully divides this airy terrace into two more intimate areas, while retaining the sense of wide-open space.

pergolas and plant supports

The special qualities of metal come into their own when constructing three-dimensional features in the garden. Its combination of physical strength and visual lightness makes it the perfect material for plant-supporting structures.

Right: Patinated steel angle sections provide an original structural support for a broad timber rail, creating a simple and effective contemporary pergola.

Below: Screen walls of steel reinforcing mesh provide support for plants on this large pergola.

Arbours, pergolas, arches and gazebos must be strong enough to support heavy climbing plants and to withstand the extreme force of buffeting winds. When built of timber, they are necessarily stout and solid, but structures made of steel can look relatively delicate without compromising their stability.

Traditional designs in curly "wrought iron" style remain firm favourites for gardens in both town and country and can be bought ready-made or commissioned from an artist-blacksmith. These tend to look most comfortable with period houses, however; for contemporary house gardens, it is well worth checking out garden shows and magazines for some of the fresh new formats that are now available.

Tall obelisks and cone-shaped plant trainers can give an instant lift to a terrace or courtyard scheme. They make good punctuation marks, either as stand-alone features or to introduce a three-dimensional element in a planting bed. Both galvanized and rustic iron versions are available, appropriate for urban and country-style locations respectively.

Stainless steel structures introduce a clean-looking, architectural element to a cutting-edge garden scheme, particularly if they are sensitively designed to reflect the style and details of the property. The metal can be given either a satin or a shiny bright finish, each with its own character. A sleek, sweeping pergola would look sensational over a dining terrace, while an archway or tunnel could frame a staircase. Visually light materials such as glass, Perspex (Plexiglass) and nylon might be incorporated as screens or canopies, while hardwood provides a contrastingly solid form of detailing for handrails and steps. Such structures are definitely in the luxury bracket, however, and would have to be commissioned and installed by a specialist.

Above: The fantastical use of twisted wirework, exemplified in this adorable French-style confection, goes in and out of fashion, but the time and skill required to make such a piece means that such items are now rarities.

Left: This rusted steel arbour demonstrates an original use of ironwork. The contemporary feel, combined with the organic form reminiscent of a globe artichoke, is in wonderful contrast to the traditional walled kitchen garden in which it stands.

surfaces

The practicality of industrial metals is now being taken advantage of in
contemporary garden design. Brilliant stainless steel appears on terraces,
while mesh grids make elegant pathways through groves of bamboo.

Opposite: Gravel can be tiring to walk on, but an overlay of steel mesh provides an attractive, secure path.

Below: Intimacy is achieved in a formal pool with pink lighting glowing through both the shiny steel mesh walkway and the water.

Below right: Textured stainless steel sheet makes an unusual decorative cladding for this timber post.

Stainless steel in sheet form may be used in conjunction with other flooring materials. It is too costly, and perhaps too aggressive, to use *en masse*, and can become uncomfortably hot in sunlight. However, if its use is restricted to smaller areas, a slick element of brilliance can be introduced to a contemporary garden. A steel pathway cuts a real dash through a planting scheme, the differences in texture between the metal and foliage being shown up dramatically. A shiny steel contrast detail would add a glamorous touch to a hardwood deck or dark slate paving. Depending upon the desired result, smooth reflective or satin finishes are available; for a more textured effect, stainless steel sheet embossed with a raised pattern is another option.

Galvanized steel mesh, which is more traditionally found in industrial settings and on fire escapes, makes an excellent, non-slip tread for steps. Its free-draining

quality renders it eminently suitable for raised walkways, and it can also be used to give an edgy feel and secure tread to gravel paths.

Stainless steel would make a luxury, hard-working tabletop for a bold timber base, though more accessibly priced zinc, the time-honoured surface for French bar counters, is seeing renewed popularity in this role. Its resistance to corrosion makes it a practical choice for exterior use, and the original shiny finish soon weathers down to a dull matt that looks very comfortable in an outdoor situation.

Zinc's pliability makes it quite easy to handle in sheet form, a quality it has in common with copper, the luxury option. Copper has the added advantage of a colour unique among metals: naturally a warm golden brown, it starts out very shiny and bright but with exposure to moisture it quietly weathers to a glorious turquoise verdigris patina.

furniture and containers

Stainless steel, aluminium and zinc have all come to the forefront in garden furniture manufacturing in recent years. These new materials have brought with them sleek new designs and revolutionary production techniques.

Below: New materials and manufacturing techniques have transformed garden furniture. Lightweight aluminium frames combined with synthetic upholstery make it possible to create pool recliners that are both elegant and manageable.

A great deal of metal furniture currently on the market may look as if it is designed for the garden but is really intended only for indoor use. Made from unprotected steel, it is simply not rustproof, so be sure to establish its suitability for exterior use before purchasing items.

By contrast, aluminium is resistant to corrosion and extremely light, making it easy to move around. Café tables and chairs framed with featherlight, extruded tubes have become very popular. An attractive silvery metal, it works well in contemporary gardens and roof terraces; aluminium seating is often combined with weatherproof synthetic upholstery, which gives it a softer appearance and warm feel. Cast aluminium furniture is a different product altogether. Based on filigree 19th-century iron designs, though lighter in weight, it is available in a number of colours and finishes, and remains popular for traditional gardens.

Stainless steel is an expensive option for garden furniture, but, even so, some highly original designs are emerging, including swing seats and lightweight wire armchairs that bring a new look to old favourites. Stainless steel is also emerging strongly in the form of contrast detailing for hardwood furniture, usually for the framework or the arms and legs of seating. The effect is to introduce a clean, modern uplift to what have been largely traditional designs of dining chairs, tables and benches. Being durably corrosion-proof, stainless steel does not in any way compromise the weatherproof qualities of the timber.

Containers made from polished stainless steel have taken on a major role in contemporary gardens. Functional, clean-looking and expensive, they have enormous presence and make a good foil for specimen architectural plants.

Zinc provides an excellent lightweight alternative to steel, though there are many different qualities available. Some zinc containers are flimsy, with a bright shiny finish that tones down unevenly with age. The best are fitted with a second-skin liner to provide a heat-resistant air space, and are pre-treated to give a soft antique patina to the outside. Planters that are fixed in place, which are especially suited to restricted spaces such as terraces, can be constructed from marine-quality ply and then covered with zinc sheeting. Copper sheeting, useful when a warmer tone is required, can be used in the same way.

Lead has been a traditional material for plant containers for centuries, and while reproduction castings still abound, the current trend is towards simple, oversized shapes. Though it is a sturdy and corrosion-proof metal, its weight is prodigious, and it is certainly not suitable for roof gardens, areas of decking or destinations with difficult access.

Below: Reproduction designs in cast lead make elegant, stylish containers for a traditional garden.

Above: An unusual steel-clad dining table and curvaceous aluminium-framed chairs suit the cool, contemporary lines of this terrace. Metal furniture must be given a shaded position, however, to avoid burning.

Right: A wonderfully refreshing take on the traditional swing seat, this finely detailed stainless steel design appears to float on air.

sculpture and decoration

Gardens make an excellent sculpture gallery, as the planted surroundings and ever-changing play of light and shade provide the perfect setting for dramatic pieces of art, or amusing and eye-catching decorative features.

Metal sculptural decoration in the garden has been largely confined over the last few centuries to figurative castings made from either bronze or lead. Although there seems little decline in the popularity of traditional subjects, such as animals and maidens, an increasing number of artists are now creating modern pieces for the garden landscape in a much more challenging, free and organic style.

A large number of sculptors and artists are now using steel to develop exciting forms that are expressly designed to be set within the garden landscape rather than for a room indoors. Metals, with their ability to be cut, bent and welded, are a useful interpretative medium, and many unusual designs are appearing, often taking their inspiration directly from plants and trees. Sculptural fountains, often made from copper, featuring leaves and stems are very popular, as are exciting lanterns and torches.

A current trend for rusty iron is often expressed in structures of untreated steel rods, which have a certain raw and understated charm that blends well with informal planting schemes. However, Cor-ten steel is in a completely different league. Specially manufactured to take on a fabulous patina of rich browns and golds as it weathers, it is a favourite with modern artists and sculptors, especially for slab-like and monumentally scaled projects.

Several outdoor galleries specialise in outstanding modern sculpture, while flower shows and local country events are excellent sources, attracting many up-and-coming sculptors and blacksmiths.

Left: Cor-ten steel is beloved of sculptors for its massive strength and beautiful weathered texture and colouring. This dramatically slashed piece towers up to the sky.

Above: A copper gutter and rain chain provides an attractive and dynamic alternative to a drainpipe for directing water from the roof.

Left: Spiky planting and tall poles set with shiny metal balls, combined with a seating enclosure of rusting reinforcing mesh, merge into an amusingly chaotic courtyard feature that contrasts sharply with the cool façade of the house beyond.

chapter six

terracotta, ceramic & brick

Terracotta is an attractive, sensual material with a warm earthiness that suits it perfectly for use in the garden. Though mainly associated with pots, it is invaluable for a range of landscaping purposes. It is just one of a number of different products made from clay, deep layers of which are deposited over large areas of the earth. Literally "baked earth", terracotta is one of the oldest manufactured materials, but its aesthetic and functional qualities remain relevant today.

Left: Classical terracotta pots combine beautifully with well-maintained topiary. They are a key feature of formal gardens, such as this sophisticated Italianate design.

Clays vary widely in character, depending upon the region and country from which they are sourced, and they may contain minerals such as iron and silica that affect the colour and texture of the finished product. They are not always the familiar burnished orange-red of typical bricks and flowerpots, but they can reflect all the lovely earthy tones from palest buff through brown, grey and black. Clay's malleability allows it to be moulded or pressed into any shape, from plant containers and other decorative objects to bricks and tiles for use in many types of construction and surfacing.

The content and structure of clay will affect the performance of the end product, but the temperature at which it is fired is also crucial. Low firings result in a porous material that is unable to withstand outdoor use, whereas clay fired at high temperatures becomes hard and impermeable to water, rendering it highly resistant to frost damage.

Bricks used always to be made by hand using clay from local sources. For this reason, the character of buildings was regionally distinctive up to the middle of the 19th century. Now most bricks are machine made and widely distributed, so diffusing this regional effect. Bricks are a versatile medium appropriate for building walls and various other types of construction, and some are also suitable for flooring. Engineering bricks are the hardest and most durable. They are available in tones ranging from buff to orange/brown and black, some of which can be quite harsh. The more mellow deep purplish black is one of the most attractive colours, and is especially suitable for work in a contemporary setting. For gardens of period houses and country-style schemes, the earthy texture and tonal variations of handmade bricks give them an advantage over factory-made products. The former are much more expensive, but it is sometimes possible to source old reclaimed bricks as a cheaper alternative.

Opposite: Handmade bricks have a unique quality and texture. This low retaining wall combines a mixture of colours, ranging from deep red to black, with a simple bond pattern to create a deliberately rustic effect.

Right: Terracotta pots and exotic agaves combine to give a play of textures and styles, and make a strong structural statement with the lovely "arts and crafts" wall.

Far right: The surface of unglazed terracotta paviours takes on a rich patina with age.

Right: A classic use of ceramic is mosaic. Intricate patterns can be created, and it is a good way to introduce colour into the garden.

Far right: Handmade bricks are used as a laying detail with riven sandstone paviours.

Right: A terracotta oil jar makes the perfect foil for blooming summer planting.

Far right: Brickwork paving can be laid in many geometric patterns and will pick up considerable charm as it weathers.

Far left: Tough engineering bricks are used here to build a flight of steps.

Left: Ceramic tiles can be used to create an almost limitless number of designs and patterns, although only specially manufactured exterior tiles should be used in the garden.

Far left: Attractive and unusual flooring designs can be made using ceramic pieces in a mosaic pattern.

Left: These beautifully coloured clay paviours have all the rustic appeal of 19th-century country houses.

Far left: Moulded clay coping tiles are used to edge a shallow pool.

Left: Clay's malleability enables it to take any shape. These hand-made spheres have been fired to achieve a textured patina.

floors, steps and paths

Paving and groundwork in the garden have the same importance as parquet or tiled floors indoors. Clay tiles provide a practical surface and an uncluttered background against which furniture, decoration and planting can stand out.

Opposite: Reminiscent of an Arabian palace, this path is made of richly coloured tiles in traditional patterns.

Right: Golden terracotta adds warmth to dark green planting.

Below: Dark bricks define the eccentric shape of this terrace.

Tiling provides a convenient and attractive method of covering floor surfaces. The wide range of sizes and shapes offers good flexibility in layout, and there are choices of colour, texture and finish to suit any design scheme. Tiles are perfect for terraces and small courtyards and particularly valuable for awkward situations such as narrow paths and steps. They can also provide a visual link with the house when matching tiles are used in a room that opens on to the garden. Paviours and floor tiles are available in a wide range of earth tones, from pale buff through to browns and blacks. Finishes vary from smooth to rough, and this is a worthwhile consideration if the area is in danger of becoming slippery.

Floor tiles are usually plain, and simple layouts generally prove the most effective. However, details in a contrasting pattern, colour or tile size can make a good visual break in a large expanse of floor. Decorative borders can frame a plain terrace or path, while panel insets create distinctive focal points. It is possible to source beautifully coloured tiles for use in mosaics and other exotic patterns, but you should always ensure that they are suitable for exterior use.

Terracotta has been valued since Roman times for its warm, inviting qualities. Handmade terracotta tiles have a lovely texture, and their slightly uneven surfaces combine to make a very attractive floor that is rustic yet sophisticated. They come in a wide colour range, from very pale, which looks particularly effective when set off by a relief of deep-toned insets, to deeper shades. The latter are often found with a distinctive brindled effect that tends to look best laid alone. Machine-made tiles are a cheaper option. They are usually smoother, with less character, but their regularity of shape makes for easy laying. When selecting terracotta tiles, remember that many are

low-fired and porous, making them totally unsuitable for exterior use, so check for their frost resistance and general suitability before ordering. They frequently need to be sealed to protect against water penetration and staining.

Simulated terracotta tiles, made from tinted cement, are economically priced and very hardwearing. Because of their regular size and shape, they are also convenient to lay.

Vitrified clay quarry tiles may also be considered as a durable, less expensive, alternative to terracotta, though they lack its character and textural subtlety. Because they are non-porous, their functionality is excellent for utility paving, and their red, brown and black colours give them a suitably low-key appearance. Fully vitrified brick paviours are much more handsome. They are very tough and can be obtained with a secure, non-slip finish suitable for steps and all kinds of groundworks.

Tiling is skilled work, best left to the professional. Tiles must always be laid on a firm concrete base, and thick paving tiles should be set in wet cement.

Bricks are fairly easy to lay on a well-prepared bed of hardcore, sand and cement. Care needs to be taken when selecting them, as most bricks are made for walling and are therefore too crumbly for use on the ground, unless you are intending to achieve a vintage effect. It is best to take advice from your supplier on a suitable type for your needs.

Brick flooring is very suggestive of period country gardens, though it can work well in an urban environment too. Dark engineering bricks work brilliantly in contemporary gardens. Their small scale is especially suited to intimate areas such as courtyards, while brick paths make efficient linking or dividing devices among areas of planting. A number of attractive patterns can be achieved with bricks, including basketweave – a slightly busy design that tends to make spaces seem smaller – and herringbone, which is relaxing to the eye and has a gentle directional slant that works well for paths and larger terraces. Borders and blocks of brick pattern can also be combined effectively with stone or cement paviours in the form of contrasting detail to add interest to a bland area.

Above: Terracotta tiles laid like bright stepping stones among the creeping greenery make an attractive, informal garden pathway.

Left: Warm red brick steps lead irresistibly to a romantic timber clapboard house. Note the edging, which is correctly detailed with bricks set lengthways.

Opposite: Decorative tiles turn these steps into a linking feature between the house and pool.

walls and constructions

It is the greatest desire of many people to have a garden enclosed by walls, and it is hard to deny that bricks – elegant, warm in colour and texture and sympathetic in scale – are the most attractive medium from which to build them.

Below: Texture is one of the most important elements in the hard landscaping of a courtyard or small garden. Sandstone paving reflects the tone and texture of the high brick wall in this courtyard setting, and the combination forms a blank canvas for the details of the courtyard, such as the furniture, containers and planting.

Bricks are an extremely versatile building material with a comfortable domestic scale and character. They are made to a standard size, and, due to their rectangular shape, they can be arranged in interlocking patterns to build vertical constructions of differing thicknesses.

The overall look of the finished work is controlled by the different laying patterns, which are known as bonds. English bond, the classic design for a garden wall, is created by alternating pairs of bricks laid side by side lengthways (stretchers) with others set on end (headers). The resulting wall combines strength with an elegant and interesting pattern. There are many traditional bonds, and it is worth looking at built structures to see how much more distinguished some of the older, more complex patterns can be than the plain stretcher-style bond that is used today.

Freestanding walls can make beautiful garden boundaries and may also be used as divisions within the garden, to highlight a particular area or to create suspense by concealing a view. Brick walls also make very good supports for climbing plants: they retain a lot of heat from the sun, encouraging the growth of more tender climbers and espaliered fruit trees. This is the practical reason behind the construction of walled kitchen gardens in old country estates.

It is always important to respect the surrounding architecture when selecting construction materials for garden use. Care should be taken when choosing bricks to ensure that both their colour and the nature of the material will be in keeping. Brick and terracotta seldom combine well with creamy stone houses, for example. If you are thinking of building walls near an old brick-built house, consider using second-hand bricks, which have more character than new ones, and can be obtained from specialist suppliers to match the existing brickwork building.

Bricks are an ideal medium for built features in the garden. Their size and shape give them enormous flexibility, making it possible to create curves and complex forms. If the garden is on a sloping site, changes of level can be accommodated by constructing retaining walls to hold back the earth. Steps of varying height, width and depth are simple to achieve using brick. The small size of each element enables the construction of complex flights of straight, angled or curving stairs.

All kinds of round or rectangular structures can be built from brick. A formal raised pond for fish or water lilies, a wall fountain or more complex water features including multi-level cascades are all possible. Slate or stone copings and the careful choice of surrounding floor details will give a professional finish.

Small gardens benefit enormously from built-in features, which save space and keep the area looking uncluttered. Incorporating a brick-built barbecue and fitted bench seating in a patio design makes an excellent entertaining area, and is a particular boon in a tiny courtyard. Brick benches with removable timber lids can double as storage boxes for tools and garden supplies to save even more space.

Square brick piers make excellent supporting columns for a pergola or entrance gates. Though more difficult to construct, a circular brick pillar supporting a planted urn makes an extremely distinctive stand-alone feature.

Glazed ceramic tiles come into their own in the garden for special decorative effects. Their dazzling range of colours permits the creation of dramatic and eye-catching patterns that are especially relevant in gardens with tropical and Mediterranean themes. Tiles are eminently suitable for covering any surface,

Above: This curved freestanding wall creates a boundary between parts of the garden and provides warmth and shelter for the tender perennials in front of it.

Right: Brick is a very versatile material for all kinds of construction: rectangular shapes are straightforward, and it is also possible to create curving walls, such as this round pool.

including walls, screens and tabletops, while single decorative panels provide interesting features to relieve plain rendered walls or screens. There is plenty of scope for creating exciting designs in dramatic combinations of colour, perhaps using broken tiles to "paint" a picture in mosaic.

Features such as fountains and benches built from basic blockwork can be transformed by facing them with coloured tiles. Curved objects such as formal raised pools present no problem with this treatment, and it is even possible to create fantastical sculptures decorated with small pieces of broken tile.

Coloured tiles look very effective combined with water and they are frequently used to line fountains and swimming pools, for which they are an attractive, hardwearing and hygienic solution. Any size can be used, though mosaic tiles are popular for intricate designs. These tiny pre-cut shapes, which must be specified for outdoor use, are especially suited to creating patterns and covering curved surfaces. Soft blues and greens work very well, but as colours tend to look brighter under water, you should be careful when choosing tiles for a large expanse like a pool, or the result can be unnaturally vivid.

Exterior construction work is a serious matter, and large brick structures, especially high walls, which are potentially dangerous, must be built with extreme care. Deep, sound foundations are needed, and experienced bricklaying skills are required to achieve a smooth and elegant finish. Added to this, the cost of materials is not inconsiderable, so it is advisable to leave this work to a professional.

Tiling is a skilled job, best left to the professional where large areas are involved. The tiles must always be laid on a sound, firm base such as a concrete screed and fixed with a suitable waterproof adhesive. Remember that only fully vitrified tiles can be used outside, and, if in doubt, check with your supplier.

Above: A serene marble fountain, set upon a plinth of mosaic, dominates this Islamic-style courtyard. The colourful and detailed mosaic evokes the design of an exotic Arabian carpet.

Right: Here decorative tiles have been used to provide relief to this concrete screen.

Opposite: Silver lustre mosaic tiles shimmer in reflection in this exotic stylized fountain.

containers

Clay has been used to make pots and containers since the very beginning of civilization, and terracotta's most notable use for gardeners is the manufacture of flowerpots, the most beautiful of which are produced by hand.

Right: Glazed clay pots integrated within the planting bring reflective qualities to the garden.

Below: Old terracotta oil jars make excellent focal points among naturalistic planting.

The most famous and sought-after terracotta pots come from Impruneta in the Tuscan region of Italy, where the clay deposits are extremely fine and dense. Modern plant pots are made in many regions of the world, and though they may look as if they come from the Mediterranean, they may actually have arrived from China.

Traditional designs, sometimes festooned with swags of fruit or flowers, or modelled on curving amphorae, remain firm favourites, but simpler forms are beginning to overtake them in popularity. Big, bold round pots with heavy-banded rims look wonderful planted with specimen palms or olive trees, as the textures and colours of both container and plant are reminiscent of warm climates. Square or rectangular containers can be planted with neatly clipped topiary to complement their form. Oversized modern containers in dramatically simple shapes work brilliantly in contemporary settings and look particularly effective in formal groups.

Natural, unglazed terracotta is porous, which is an excellent quality for plant containers. It remains cool when placed in hot sun and allows the soil to dry out slowly and naturally, avoiding the possibility of waterlogging and ensuring that there is sufficient air in the soil to keep roots healthy.

To avoid the risk of damage in cold winters, it is most important to choose terracotta containers that are guaranteed frostproof, which means that they have been fired in the kiln to at least 1,000 degrees C (1,800 degrees F). If the pots are cracked, water from the soil will penetrate, causing them to break when it freezes, so these should always be emptied at the end of summer to avoid this possibility. Glazed terracotta pots, though they are often lovely to look at, are seldom suitable for outdoor use.

Above: Square shapes are notoriously difficult to make successfully, and these handmade pots take weeks to finish. The elegantly tall, contemporary containers are carefully balanced with a planting of low, clipped topiary.

Left: This row of hand-thrown, tall clay urns are raised on a tile-clad plinth to make a striking statement without any need for plants.

chapter seven

new materials

Creating a garden is a vibrant and exhilarating process, one that is active in the present and emerging from, rather than fixed on, ideas from the past. As the garden is part of the human environment, it follows that fashions there will keep pace with other areas of life. Developments in technology bring with them new design styles and materials, and the garden is an ideal stage on which to create fun, surprise or even shock.

Left: Startling design concepts are always to be found at the annual Chaumont Garden Festival in France. This sweeping tunnel, formed from hoops of thin plastic film, creates vibrant effects of colour and light that change with the sun.

new materials introduction

Throughout the centuries, and with each changing phase of architectural taste, gardens have been places in which to display new ideas in design and fabrication. This century brings with it the benefits of increasingly sophisticated manufacturing processes and a broad range of durable and attractive synthetic materials that have been developed and improved over the past few decades for interior or industrial applications. Now is the time for some of these to take their place out of doors in the garden.

Synthetic materials offer many advantages for outdoor use, both decorative and practical. Lightweight and waterproof, they can be spun into textiles for upholstery, parasols and canopies, injection-moulded to make garden furniture and planting containers or formed into sheets for glazing. Even old supermarket carrier bags are being recycled into benches – not so beautiful, but eco-friendly.

Visually, the most important contribution of plastics is colour, and every possible hue and tone can be achieved: clear and brilliant oranges and reds, pinks and purples, blues, greens and yellows. The colours of these modern materials will not fade, and though overuse can introduce a very artificial effect in the garden, it should be remembered that colours of this intensity do occur in nature, though they are found only in tiny amounts: in spring shoots, the petals of a flower or the wings of a butterfly. *En masse*, they inject freshness and vitality, aligning well with play areas and spaces dedicated to children. However, play is not restricted to childhood, and splashes or even pools of brilliance introduce excitement and animation to a forward-looking, contemporary garden. The practicalities of synthetics are equally available to those with more restrained tastes, as the new materials are also produced in neutral tones that blend very well with sophisticated and understated designs.

Opposite: Perspex (Plexiglass) is available in an enormous range of colours. It can be cut to any shape, is translucent and won't shatter like glass. To achieve an unusual sculptural effect, it is easy to make rectangular pillars such as these by fixing the joints with an appropriate weatherproof adhesive.

Right: The surface of this unusual resin sculpture closely ties in with the shape of the surrounding plants.

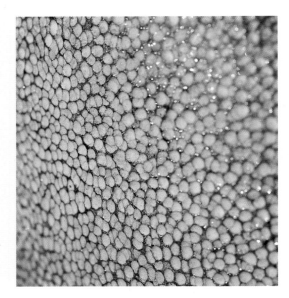

Far right: The patinated finish of this cast resin gives an interesting surface texture.

Right: Weatherproof woven plastic is increasingly being used to make garden furniture.

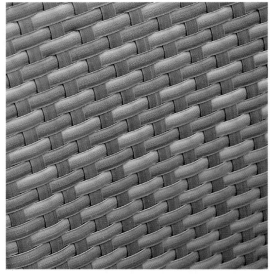

Far right: The ultra-smooth surface of this plastic has a wonderful translucent quality.

Right: Resin can be combined with other materials, such as bronze, and moulded into sensual shapes, as in this fabulous chair.

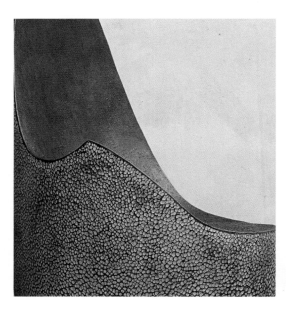

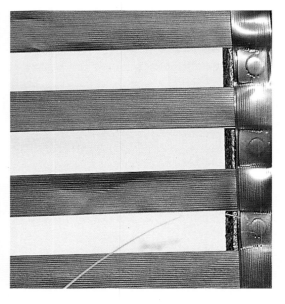

Far right: Industrial materials can often be put to new uses in the garden. This immensely strong, tough baler tape has been used to make an effective screen.

Far left: A bright red plastic canopy casts a dramatic shadow as the sun streams through its translucent material.

Left: Recycling is now a part of everyday life, so why not use car tyre treads as paving, here set in a bed of marble chippings.

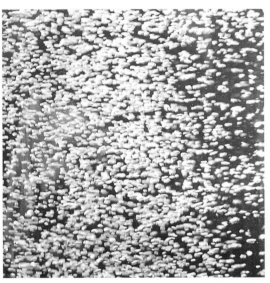

Far left: A bubble effect can be given to plastics during production to add interest to hard landscaping features.

Left: A good choice for table-tops in a modern setting, reinforced plastics are strong and water-resistant, making them ideal for colourful canopies and covers.

Far left: Plastic-coated wooden poles give colour and impact.

Left: This adjustable sunscreen, made of waterproof fabric supported on horizontal wires, demonstrates a novel design concept.

modern materials

Plastics have in the past been associated with shoddiness, but they have now totally outgrown that derelict image through production techniques that have developed products of amazing technical sophistication and versatility.

Below: This design is based on a section through a plant stem. Vertical rubber pipes represent the vessels through which water and nutrients flow, while tall wire mesh cylinders give support for young succulents. Rubber particles represent the soil.

Plastic is in fact a generic term; it can refer to a huge range of materials that vary enormously in appearance, performance and price. Those most relevant to garden use include Perspex (Plexiglass), an acrylic material that can be moulded into solid shapes or formed into flat sheets, and polycarbonate, a lightweight alternative that is more scratch-resistant and is suitable for glazing. Polypropylene can be injection moulded and was made famous in the 1960s by Robin Day's then revolutionary stacking chairs, which have now become an integral part of everyday life. Teflon is best known for its use as a non-stick lining for kitchenware, but it is also used as a waterproofing coating for textiles, most famously for the London Millennium Dome.

Plastics can be soft, bendable, rigid or liquid, transparent, opaque, translucent, coloured, patterned, processed into textiles and paints or moulded into shapes, to suit whatever purpose is required. The end products are immensely practical, being lightweight, waterproof and weather resistant. Fears about colour fading and surface deterioration are largely outdated. They always tend to look new, which is perhaps not always desirable in the garden.

Rubber is a natural material that is beginning to make an appearance outside. Its main benefits are its soft, yielding qualities, making it much in demand for children's play areas. Its high cost and scarcity has led to the development of interesting synthetic alternatives. Synthetic rubber sheet with a raised stud profile is a useful, non-slip floor covering for a terrace and is also appropriate for play spaces.

Astroturf is recognized as a tough, low-maintenance sports surface and is now beginning to appear in small gardens where natural lawns are inappropriate. Popular with both children and parents, it provides a fresh green surface that can withstand any amount of wear and tear, or simply look green all year round with the minimum of attention.

Above: Here plastic-covered wooden garden hoes dominate a section of this garden, providing a humorous wave of colour.

Right: Translucent "bubble effect" Perspex columns provide visually neutral support for the curved plastic "wave" canopy and inject a sense of graceful movement to the underwater theme.

boundaries and screens

The type of boundary chosen will depend on many factors: opaque boundaries will provide privacy; translucent ones will give protection from the wind without blocking the view, while arches can frame a focal point.

Transparency is one of the greatest qualities of Perspex (Plexiglass), making it an ideal material wherever separation is required without blocking out light or view. It is available completely clear or in brilliant, jewel-bright colours.

Clear Perspex is as shatter resistant and tough as plastic, and it is often used in place of toughened glass to screen a balcony from wind, though the benefits of lighter weight and easier handling must be offset against its vulnerability to scratching. However, it is in its brilliant colours that Perspex really comes into its own as a decorative material. Possessing the qualities of stained glass without its fragility, Perspex can be clear and jewel-like or opaque and mysterious.

Endlessly exciting graphic effects can be achieved using panels cut from sheet material. Geometric shapes can be used as insets to relieve a plain rendered wall or set along the top in adjoining panels. In a large garden, where there is sufficient space, monolithic panels can be fixed into the ground like glowing sentinels, to capture the effects of moving sunlight. A courtyard can be brought to life after dark with a huge vertical light box. Small, coloured light boxes can even be incorporated into an open slatted timber screen to enliven a sheltered seating space.

A sense of discovery is desirable in even the smallest garden. A screen is a valuable device to foil an opening or bring an element of seclusion to a covered dining area. Make a lively retro curtain, reminiscent of a clinking, Courrèges frock, by connecting small discs of Perspex with metal rings and hang it to screen off a private part of the garden.

Simple screening effects can be achieved by stretching synthetic textiles across a timber framework. This versatile system, which can be made up of individual panels, is useful in urban locations and exposed areas, such as roof terraces. The textiles can be fixed vertically, diagonally or horizontally to provide privacy or shelter from sun and wind. For a less formal solution, a sail-like canopy makes an effective shield from the weather and a good privacy barrier, with the triangular shape providing a sweeping dynamic. It can be slung from a wall and stretched tight with ropes tied to bolts in the ground.

Opposite: The steel frame of this screen is inset with an acrylic panel laminated with reflective film to create a shimmering surface.

furniture and containers

The plastic chair has really grown up since the emergence of its flimsy white prototype. Superior materials and manufacturing techniques have produced a new generation of sophisticated designs to suit all tastes, in both fun colours and cool neutral tones.

Below: New woven plastics are taking over the garden furniture industry. Completely weatherproof and excellent mimics of natural cane, these materials open up – at long last – the possibility of using comfortable armchairs out of doors.

Stackable dining chairs are immensely practical, allowing furniture to be stored in winter, and are easily portable for mixed indoor and outdoor use. The new solid moulded designs have a chic elegance, while lighter-looking forms combine steel or aluminium legs with rigid synthetic seating shells.

It's always good to retain a sense of humour in the garden, and plastics are the ideal materials for visual jokes. Occasional seating is taking on a space-age sculptural appearance with injection-moulded, rigid plastic pods looking like slightly squashed puffballs, while erotic red sofas leave little to the imagination.

Slabs of Perspex (Plexiglass) have the advantage of strength combined with an ephemeral appearance. They make functional tabletops and benches with a feeling of fantasy and might create visually fragile swing seats, suspended from steel wire rope.

Synthetic fibres make excellent hardwearing textiles for outdoor seating. They are most often used as a single layer stretched on an aluminium framework for folding recliners and loungers that are extremely light and easy to move around. As these fabrics are free-draining and dry quickly, they are particularly appropriate for furniture in pool areas.

Plastics can be moulded and formed into replicas of many natural materials, and though the results are not always successful, there is a new breed of synthetic furniture that successfully and elegantly imitates wicker sofas and armchairs. Though very expensive, it introduces a new level of comfort and classical style to the genre.

Synthetic planting containers are a boon for gardens with restricted access, and on balconies and roof gardens their light weight is an advantage. Interesting contemporary planters, moulded from PVC and other plastics, are starting to make an appearance, though the widest choice is to be found in glass-reinforced resin. This is light, strong and can be made to resemble a number of natural materials including terracotta, stone, lead and bronze. Designs range from traditional reproductions to the very sleek and modern, so they can be teamed with any kind of project.

Left: This erotically suggestive red plastic "love seat" demonstrates the sculptural possibilities of this versatile material.

Below left: Well-designed plastic stacking furniture, such as these crisp white chairs, is invaluable where space is limited. It can lead a double life, inside and out.

Below: This sensuous sculptural seating is made from solid bronze resin with a special surface finish.

chapter eight

organic

The constraints and pressures of daily life, with

its tight schedules, cramped commuting and

the stressful effect of being subject to constant

noise, can lead to a desire to opt out entirely

from the rat race. This is seldom practicable,

but at least at home in the garden it is possible

to react against the norm and create a restorative

refuge, where nature rules and organic forms

and materials are dominant.

Left: In a wonderful example of freedom of organic expression, a
seething mass of young shoots (also known as teaspoons) pushes
up the earth to reach daylight, while a boardwalk entices the
onlooker to investigate the hidden depths.

By relaxing ideas about form and structure, it is possible to make a pleasingly unconventional, untamed garden, using natural, unfinished materials that, instead of being arranged along conventional lines, are allowed to follow their own natural rhythm and shape. In this wilder, less restrictive kind of garden, birds and insects find havens for nesting among twigs and vines, with watering holes nearby for refreshment. The calming and introspective effect extends to humans, too, of course, and there should be space for generous rustic seating and fascinating sculptural effects.

It is always interesting to interpret conventional design ideas using materials that are normally associated with an entirely different use. A funky, contemporary interpretation might contrast organic materials with a very strict, modern design. This kind of garden can take an off-beat theme, and might utilize unexpected materials for constructions, as well as incorporating quirky decorative details made from so-called "found objects".

With a lateral mind and an eye for shape and texture, a whole world of reclaimed materials can be re-created into sculptural forms, which are all the more pleasing for the release of personal inventiveness they can inspire. Driftwood provides rich pickings, often taking on surprising anthropomorphic forms that can be incorporated into themed set-pieces. It is also well worth keeping your eyes and ears open near construction sites and skips for the possibility of useful pieces of construction materials. Generous slabs of timber, such as old house beams, make excellent building blocks. Clearance sales and classified advertisements can also yield booty, such as old factory floors and disused railway sleepers (ties). Specialist reclamation dealers are always a good source of unusual building materials. Though often pricey, they offer the advantages of a wide choice and the facility to deliver to site.

Opposite: Natural materials lend themselves readily to sculptural devices. Slung across an overgrown pond on lengths of fishing net, this "bridge" is draped with a seething tangle of weed-infested sisal, looking like an escaped sea monster.

Right: Exotic vines like these are among the many stems that can be woven and used as decorative construction materials.

Far right: Unpeeled twigs such as hazel, cornus and willow can be nailed to supports to create screens and barriers.

Right: Wooden clothes pegs, patiently drilled and connected by keyrings, make a novel approach to screening.

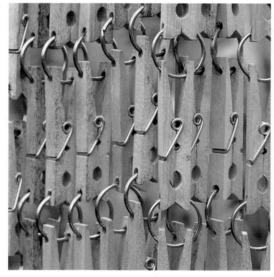

Far right: A rusty old rail truck provides the perfect backdrop to tufts of free-flowing golden grasses.

Right: Driftwood is piled high to form a textural rustic pillar.

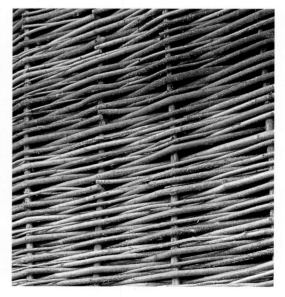

Far right: Woven willow makes excellent screening from wind.

Far left: Straw, hessian and sisal string set an organic tone in the garden and are useful for set-dressing.

Left: Steel gabions don't always have to be filled with stones and rock; this log pile demonstrates a less hostile approach.

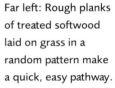

Far left: Rough planks of treated softwood laid on grass in a random pattern make a quick, easy pathway.

Left: Recycled teaspoons are one of the everyday items that can be introduced into a free-form design.

Far left: Traditional apple storage racks also have a decorative function.

Left: Pieces of rope and string add a nautical touch and make interesting details around the garden.

groundwork

Making one's way through an organic garden should feel like a textural exploration, with timber boardwalks pushing their way through wild grasses and logs bridging gushing streams as if they have simply fallen into place.

Right: Rusting metal washers can be used to add textural detail to a small area of floor.

Below: Horizontal sections sliced through an old tree trunk make a sympathetic rustic pathway through the garden planting.

Landscapes of rough grass demand an informal trail rather than a paved path. Rough, seasoned planks make a textural surface that contrasts well with the fresh green background and is both stylish and easy to walk on. For a natural effect, range pieces of different sizes and shapes in an irregular, flowing pattern that moves with the contours of the land. Circular log slices sawn from a fallen tree provide an alternative method of making a path in grass, creating the effect of stepping-stones. Arrranging them in a meandering fashion rather than a straight line suits their informal look. The timbers can be positioned directly in the ground after they have been treated with preservative, though it is preferable to use gravel or compacted hardcore as a base. Ensure that the finished surface of the wood lies beneath the height of mower blades so the area can be maintained easily.

Chipped bark, normally supplied for mulching, makes a cheap surfacing for paths and walkways and helps to suppress weeds. Its dark brown colour is natural and unobtrusive and it is light and easy to handle. Heavy, woven jute or sisal, normally sold for interior carpeting, is a possibility in areas of little or no traffic. It makes an interesting contrast with planting and will also suppress weeds. When it eventually rots down, it can be covered with a new layer.

Hard aggregates such as chippings, pebbles, sand and even coal can be used for surfacing. Think laterally about industrial and domestic leftovers too, such as metal washers, steel filings, teaspoons or broken terracotta. Success lies in the presentation, so arrange them like works of art, not garbage.

Opposite: Free-form design needs to be safe: this attractively haphazard walkway of random planks and posts is firmly footed into concrete foundations.

raised beds and steps

A series of terraces can add enormous visual and spatial appeal to tricky sites such as long, narrow gardens or those with steep slopes. Raised beds add dimension to small gardens and allow cultivation where soil levels are low.

Right: Railway sleepers (ties) make effective steps in this small courtyard garden.

Below: Large round wooden poles form a retaining wall to this raised bed.

Both raised beds and terraces entail constructing retaining walls. These can be very costly to build traditionally in brick or stone, but in an organic treatment, where the look should be informal with a sense of freedom, they can be achieved simply with very effective results.

Whole sections of young tree trunks, with their irregularities of shape and texture, look really interesting and very much part of the landscape. They can be arranged horizontally to contain a low bed but are perhaps best lined up vertically to create retaining walls. Specialist timber merchants can supply them, but if sourcing proves difficult, round poles sold for fencing posts can be used.

Railway sleepers (ties) are exceptionally strong and versatile and their rectilinear shape aids construction. They can be hard to cut and because they are very heavy they must have good concrete foundations; steel bolts and ties give additional security. They may be arranged horizontally, one above the other, for a shallow bed, but set on end, side by side, sections of sleepers make sturdy retaining walls.

Rustic-style steps can be created by using heavy sections of timber for the risers. With their substantial weight and stability, sleepers provide well-proportioned, ready-to-go "building blocks", while whole round, rustic logs do a similar job, though slightly more informally. These are perhaps best used to retain a shallow flight of deep steps, which can be surfaced with contrasting gravel or wood chip.

Opposite: A raised boardwalk is an excellent way to navigate a wild or wet garden. Ensure that the timber is strong enough to take the weight of traffic, and set it securely in concrete footings.

boundaries and screens

The natural texture required for informal fencing can be achieved using one of the new woven materials, which may be purchased by the roll. Alternatively, you could weave a screen of reeds or bamboo, or plant fresh willow withies.

Below: Screening need not block a view, but can serve merely as a delineation of space. Here, rustic poles act as supports for the steel wires that surround the beds almost invisibly.

Fencing on a roll is cheap, versatile and good looking. Made from heather, reed or split bamboo, which has been securely woven together with wire, it is flexible and very easy to erect. Its understated appearance blends subtly into the background, and it combines exceptionally well with loose, informal planting. It also makes very good lightweight screening for roof terraces and balconies, providing instant privacy, and it is an efficient diffuser for wind and sunshine.

Heavy woven hurdles are made following an ancient craft tradition that is currently undergoing a revival in new rustic gardens. They are made by weaving willow withies through a strong framework of hazel uprights and are supplied in panels of various sizes. They are expensive but are beautifully finished, sometimes woven into different patterns. For a cheaper, more rustic look, choose a version woven with split hazel. Order them direct from the makers at country shows or through classified advertisements. Some craftsmen will undertake special commissions for custom designs to be built on site, but before investing too much, it is worth remembering that the lifespan of these materials is only a few years.

Alternatively, you can plant a "living willow" fence, which will continue to grow as a permanent feature, sprouting fresh leaves each spring. All you have to do is push freshly cut withies diagonally into the ground and weave them together into a firm framework. Maintenance is minimal: just a clip in autumn to keep it in shape. Fresh withies can be bought at shows in early spring or ordered directly from a grower.

All kinds of dried materials suitable for making into boundary features are available. Slim golden reeds, bought from thatching specialists, can be tied into bundles with dark coloured string, to make elegant Japanese-style fencing and screens. Bamboo can be bought from garden centres in a variety of heights and thicknesses for making rigid screens and plant supports; fix the canes with carefully made matching knots tied together at the crossing points. Flexible willow is sometimes available grown from different species that yield purple, orange or yellow stems to add a coloured dimension to a design. The stems can be woven through tall hazel sticks to make screens, fences and wigwam-style plant supports.

Above: In a new take on the garden washing line, this very effective curtain screen is made from hundreds of wooden clothes pegs.

Far left: Corn cobs, sandwiched between wire mesh, screen a cotton-lined walkway.

Left: Bales of hay, surrounded by reinforced glass provide unusual bench structures.

structures

Free up your mind and think Robinson Crusoe. With little more than a tangle of vines, some pieces of driftwood and a vivid imagination, you can create a fantastical structure that will please you and all the other local wildlife.

String and rope made from natural hemp have gorgeous textural qualities and make wonderful aids to organic construction. Varying in thickness and strength, they are suitable for making a range of dramatic features. Adults and children alike will appreciate a simple swing made from lengths of stout rope knotted through holes at each end of a good, smooth wooden plank. If hung from a tree, it makes a piece of sculpture, too, though a pergola would provide support where a tree is not available.

Rope ladders can be made by knotting together rungs of thick dowelling or sections of fence paling. Suspend rope ladders from a tree or high wall and use them as jungle-inspired plant supports for climbing vines. Ropes knotted in a fishing-net-style can

Above: Ancient trees provide an excuse to rig up a simple rope swing on which to while away the hours.

Left: An attractive inhabited dovecote introduces an air of romance and intimacy to the garden.

be made into organic boundaries or screens, plant trainers and hammocks, or can be used to form part of a climbing frame in a children's adventure area.

As a more permanent garden structure, a retreat can be anything from a quiet studio in which to write or paint, to a potting shed or a place to entertain. It can be completely enclosed from the weather, or it can have the character of a secluded courtyard or terrace. Whatever their purpose, the best hideaways look as if they have been there forever.

For the forester look, a framework cut from wind-damaged trees and clad with split logs would make a good basic shell, to which a shady veranda supported by branched tree trunks could be added. Roof it with overlapping shingles – small discs or rectangles of sawn timber – or try a reed or brushwood thatch.

For real "outback" style, finish the walls with mismatched, faded planks and make the roof from discarded sheets of corrugated metal. Any combination of driftwood, woodland cuttings, sawn softwood, twisted vines and ropes will do. Really, anything goes when creating such a playhouse – make it just as wild as you like. The only proviso is that it should be safely and sturdily constructed, and be wind and watertight. On the other hand, however untamed it looks on the surface, there is no reason why it should not be fitted with every modern convenience inside: heating, lighting, even water and cooking facilities. A shaded veranda outside, with a barbecue and a swing seat, will complete a retreat designed to invite you to stray into the garden.

Organic modernists could choose rudimentary hi-tech and build a retreat from gabions filled with oversized stones. Though rigid in form, the mass of stone has a raw, compelling attraction that suggests contained energy and nature exposed.

Above: Gabions, normally associated with civil engineering, seem to have become synonymous with new garden design. These, filled with attractive flint cobbles, have been cleverly incorporated into the arbour structure to form a seating area and raised planters.

furniture and ornament

Somewhere comfortable to while away languid hours watching the birds and listening to the sounds of nature; furniture in the organic garden should seem to appear from out of the ground, as part of the landscape, not imposed upon it.

Right: An old wooden ladder is turned into organic sculpture when decorated with a fringe of rusty garden nails.

Below: This charming group of truly organic furniture is created by training *Ligustrum jonandrum* over wirework frames.

Benches and chairs set at strategic points in the garden provide good focal points and necessary resting places, but they do not need to be highly sophisticated in terms of design and construction. Bark-covered logs, willow, chestnut and hazel are traditional materials for organic furniture, which can be woven and nailed together into quirky forms. These tend not to be overly comfortable or to have great lasting power, but they do make wonderful decoration and talking points.

Simpler in form but more enduring in performance, seats and tables can be built from substantial rustic poles and will last for years if constructed strongly.

Where something sturdier and more practical is required, a boldly impressive table with bench seats built from heavy slabs of green oak would make both a strong visual statement and a very agreeable gathering-place for meals. The most pleasing forms are often the simplest, created from thick, straight sections of timber built on a square frame.

Benches make good decorative features in their own right; a single long seat fashioned with flowing, sensuous curves would look magnificent, combining a dramatic sculptural statement with a congenial place to stop and reflect.

Ornamental furniture can be literally grown out of the ground to bring an organic effect to the garden. Living willow wands, planted directly into the soil in the early spring, can be woven into chairs or sheltering arbours, which will continue to sprout new green shoots each year. Free-form living willow sculptures are easy to create by twining long stems into shapes, and can be altered every season to take account of the growth pattern of the plants. Saplings of slim growing trees can also be treated in this way to form arches or more complicated love knots.

Topiary shapes take a long time to grow but bring sophisticated natural ornamentation to the garden. Any form is possible, from birds and animals to rowing boats, enabling themed living sculptures to be created. Chairs around a table demonstrate the versatility of this amusing art. Though normally created with evergreen box, yew or miniature privet, all of which are expensive to buy and slow to grow, a wire framework can be trained with green-leaved ivy, quickly achieving the desired result.

Decoration in the garden can come from any source. It is fun to collect wind-fallen or washed-up objects on a woodland or seashore walk, so long as no ecological damage is done. The garden, too, in winter, reveals all kinds of vine-like strands, including willow, dogwood, bramble and ivy, that can be woven into objects or free-form shapes. A collection of shells or stones can be assembled into pleasing forms or strung into garlands to hang from a veranda or tree.

Above: A thoughtful arrangement of flattened pebbles transforms them into an eyecatching organic sculptural form.

Right: A huge vase woven from reeds cleverly mimics the form of the adjacent tree fern.

water features

Water brings life to the world and demands a place in the natural garden for the sake of all the creatures living there. Whether you have space for a huge pond or just a shallow bowl, abundant wildlife will be drawn to use it.

Opposite: This naturalistic pond is carefully sited to link the garden with the glorious coastal landscape beyond it.

Below: Weathered timbers set in sand and gravel give a gentle approach to the water's edge.

Informal water features such as ponds or, more ambitiously, moving streams and waterfalls fit perfectly into an organic theme, but setting them in a natural landscape requires a sensitive touch. They need some sort of border and an approach from the rest of the garden. An appealing walkway that meshes the water margin with surrounding rough grass can be made with weathered driftwood in a bed of smooth pebbles. A shallow beach of loose stones allows birds to reach the water's edge and makes a satisfactory crunching noise under foot. There are many other ways of incorporating charismatic pieces of timber in a water garden. A heavy board or split log bridge can span a small stream to connect different parts of the garden. A pontoon platform of wooden planks overhanging a large pond is a great spot to sit. For security, it should be supported on posts bedded into a concrete base during the pond construction.

Water features can be constructed relatively simply with a flexible liner and pump. A gently bubbling spring spouting through pebbles is a lovely device where space is limited, set in a quiet spot where birds can gather to drink and bathe. It can be run by a small submersible pump in a water reservoir in the form of a plastic garbage bin sunk in the ground. A layer of pebbles, through which the water emerges, is supported by a sheet of steel mesh on the surface. An extended area of pebbles spread around it naturalizes the effect, especially when combined with simple marginal plants such as variegated grasses and iris.

More ambitious schemes such as ponds and streams require planning to ensure the right balance of water, pump and reservoir. Black PVC is one of the most popular choices of liner as it is easy to handle and economically priced, though professionals specify more expensive butyl for its strength and flexibility under all conditions. Pumps may be housed above ground or, more usually for small installations, are submersible. They divide into those designed to power fountains or waterfalls, and those capable of handling solids, which are required to work filtration systems in ponds. Large-scale schemes are best installed by professionals, though water features need not be ambitious to be successful and are great fun to make. However, very special care must be given to electricity supply when working outdoors, and it is sensible and prudent to appoint a qualified tradesman to make the connections.

index

Page numbers in italics refer to illustrations.

PICTURE CREDITS
All photography by Steven Wooster for Anness Publishing Ltd except those images listed below. In addition the publishers would like to thank the following garden designers and owners for allowing their work to be reproduced in this book:
t = top; b = bottom; l = left; r = right; c = centre
p1 Chelsea Flower Show (2002); p2 © Steven Wooster; pp4–5 © Steven Wooster/Interart Gallery; p5t (inset) Chelsea Flower Show (2003); p5c (inset) Estee Lauder garden, New York; p5b (inset) Chelsea Flower Show (2002); pp6 and 7 (inset) Luciano Giubbilei (design); p10 © Steven Wooster/ Luciano Giubbilei (design); p7 Chaumont Garden Festival (2003); p16t Hampton Court Flower Show (2003)/May & Watts Garden Design (design); p18 © Steven Wooster; p19 Chelsea Flower Show (2003)/Tom Stuart-Smith (design); p20t © Steven Wooster/Luciano Giubbilei (design); p21 'Garden from the Desert', Chelsea Flower Show (2003)/ Christopher Bradley-Hole (design); p22 t and b Chelsea Flower Show (2003)/Eric de Maeijer & Jane Hudson (design); p24t 'Sensuality', Chelsea Flower Show (2003); p24b Latchetts, UK; p25 Chaumont Garden Festival (2003); p26t Westonbirt Festival of the Garden (2003); p26b Ted Smyth (design); p27 Luciano Giubbilei (design); p28 Tatton Park Flower Show (2003)/Robert Frier at Charlesworth Design (design); p31 Chelsea Flower Show (2003)/Eric de Maeijer & Jane Hudson (design); p35 Bowles & Wyer (design); p37t Chaumont Garden Festival (2003); p37b Chelsea Flower Show; p39 Boweles & Wyer (design); p41 Bowles & Wyer (design); p42t Bowles & Wyer (design); p42b 'Serve Chilled', Tatton Park Flower Show (2003); p43t Bowles & Wyer (design); p43bl Westonbirt Festival of the Garden (2003)); p43br Westonbirt Festival of the Garden (2003); p46 © Steven Wooster/ Chelsea Flower Show (1998); p47 'Sanctuary', Tatton Park Flower Show (2003)/ Jane Mooney (design); p54 © Steven Wooster/ 'The Living Sculpture Garden', Chelsea Flower Show (2000)/ Christopher Bradley-Hole (design); © Steven Wooster/ Josie Martin (owner); p54l Tatton Park Flower Show (2003); p54r Tatton Park Flower Show (2003); p55b © Steven Wooster/Annie Wilkes (design); p58 © Didier Delmas; p59l © Steven Wooster/Luciano Giubbilei (design); p59r 'The Harbour Garden', Chelsea Flower Show (2003)/Michelle Brown (design); p60 © Steven Wooster; p61 Tatton Park Flower Show (2003); p63 © Steven Wooster/ 'Pampas: Infinity through Monotony', Chaumont Garden Festival (2001)/ Josephina Casares, Martina Barzi, Pablo Lorenzino, Thierry Lacoste, Patrick Charoin, Dries van den Brempt (design); p66t Tatton Park Flower Show (2003); p66b Chaumont Festival of the Garden (2003); p67 Chaumont Garden Festival; p68 © Steven Wooster; p69l © Steven Wooster; p69r © Steven Wooster/Ted Smyth (design); p70l Chelsea Flower Show (2003); p70r Westonbirt Festival of the Garden (2003); p71 Chelsea Flower Show (2003); p72t 'The Wrong Garden', Chelsea Flower Show (2003)/James Dyson & Jim Honey (design); p73 Westonbirt Festival of the Garden (2003); p74t © Jenny Hendy/ 'Flanade'; p74b © Steven Wooster; p75 © Steven Wooster/ 'Entre Ciel et Terre', Chaumont Garden Festival/Vincent Mayot & Thierry Nenot (design); p76t © Garden Picture Library (Gary Rogers)/ 'Mother Earth', Chelsea Flower Show (2001)/Ian Taylor (design); p76b 'The Old and the New', Chelsea Flower Show (2003)/ Pickard School of Garden Design (design); p77 © Steven Wooster/ Luciano Giubbilei (design); p78 Westonbirt Festival of the Garden (2003); p79 Chelsea Flower Show (2003); p81 Chesla Flower Show (2003); p82cl Interart Gallery; p82bl Chelsea Flower Show (2003); p83tl Interart Gallery; p83br Chelsea Flower Show (2003); p84 © Steven Wooster/ Rod Barrett & David Mitchell (design); p85l © Steven Wooster; p85r Ted Smyth (design); p86 Westonbirt Festival of the Garden (2003); p87 © Steven Wooster/Tim Feather Design (design); p88t and b Chaumont Garden Festival (2003); p89l 'An Archeologist's Urban Retreat', Hampton Court Flower Show (2003)/Sarah Lloyd (design); p89r Arley Hall, Cheshire; p90l Interart Gallery, Holland; p90r Chelsea Flower Show (2003); p91 Tatton Park Flower Show (2003)/Aedas, Mary Hoult & Ann Picot (design); p92 © Steven Wooster; p93tl Ted Smyth (design); p93b © Steven Wooster; p94 Interart Gallery, Holland; p95r Cheslea Flower Show (2003)/Mark Gregory (design); p97 Wyken Hall, UK; p99 Chelsea Flower Show (2003); p101bl Interart Gallery; p102t © Steven Wooster/ Scutt's garden, New Zealand; p102b © Steven Wooster/ Halmer Searle & Alan Bettesworth; p103 © Steven Wooster/Ross & Paula Greenville; p104 © © Steven Wooster/Ross & Paula Greenville; p105t © Steven Wooster; p105b © Steven Wooster; 'Diamond Garden'/Bowles & Wyer (design); p107t Chelsea Flower Show (2003); p107b 'Al Fresco Living', Tatton Park Flower Show (2003)/Xternal Dimensions (design); p108b © Jenny Hendy; p111t and b Luciano Giubbilei (design); p112 Chaumont Garden Festival (2003); p113 Westonbirt Festival of the Garden (2003); p114 Westonbirt Festival of the Garden (2003); p118 Westonbirt Festival of the Garden (2003); p119t Chaumont Garden Festival (2003); p119b Ellerslie Flower Show (2002); © Jenny Hendy; p121 Westonbirt Festival of the Garden (2003); p122 Maria Ornberg (design); p123t Chaumont Garden Festival (2003); p123bl Chaumont Garden Festival (2003); p123br Chelsea Flower Show (2003); p124 Chaumont Garden Festival (2003); p127 Chaumont Garden Festival (2003); p131 Chaumont Garden Festival (2003); p132 © Jenny Hendy; p133 Ellerslie Flower Show (2003); p135t Chaumont Garden Festival (2003); p135bl © Steven Wooster/ 'The Observatory', Chaumont Garden Festival/Philip Brown & Martin Lonsdale (design); p135br Westonbirt Festival of the Garden (2003); p137 Westonbirt Festival of the Garden (2003); p138t Interart Gallery; p138b © Steven Wooster/Chaumont Garden Festival (2001); p139b Westonbirt Festival of the Garden (2003); p140 'The Chattel House Garden', Chelsea Flower Show (2003)/Murdoch Wickham (design); p141 © Steven Wooster/John Gosney; p142b Chelsea Flower Show (2003); p144 Bowles & Wyer (design).

The publishers would also like to thank the following for their contributions to this book: Thérèse Lang, Bettina and Francesco Passaniti at Compact Concrete (*www.compactconcrete.com*) and John Wyer of Bowles & Wyer.

suppliers

UK

Civil Engineering Developments Ltd
728 London Road, West Thurrock, Grays
Essex RM20 3LY Tel: 01708 867 273
(stone)

Burlington Slate
www.burlingtonslate.co.uk
(slate)

Redwood Stone
The Stoneworks, West Horrington
Wells, Somerset, BA5 3EH
Tel: 01749 677777
sales@redwoodstone.co.uk
(stone)

Tom Clark
18 Church Street, Martock, Somerset
TA12 6JL Tel: 01935 822 111
(stone carving and sculpture)

Helen Sinclair
Sculpture Culture, Rhossili Farmhouse
Rhossili, Swansea SA3 1PL
Tel: 01792 390 798
(sculpture)

Fairweather Sculpture
fairweathersculpture@tinyonline.co.uk
(sculpture)

David Harber Sundials
The Sundial Workshop, Valley Farm, Bix
Henley-on-Thames, Oxfordshire,
RG9 6BW Tel: 01491 576 956
(sundials)

Partaway Aggregates
Elton Ltd, Outland Heald Quarry
Bradwell, Hope Valleys 33 9JP
Tel: 01433 621 600
(aggregates)

Windmill Aggregates
Tel: 01279 876 987
www.windmillaggregates.co.uk
(aggregates)

Solopark Plc
www.solopark.co.uk.
(reclaimed products)

LASSCO
Saint Michaels
Mark Street, London EC2A 4ER

Tel: 020 77390 448
(reclaimed products)

Brampton Willows
Upper Farm, Brampton, Beccles
Suffolk NR34 8EH Tel: 01502 575 891
(willow structures)

Marco Polo Designs
Tel: 07973 711 049
www.marko-polo.co.uk
(furniture)

Compact Concrete
www.compactconcrete.co.uk
(furniture)

Town and Country Paving
Tel: 01903 776 297
(concrete paving)

Marshalls Mono Ltd
Tel: 01422 306 300 www.marshalls.co.uk
(concrete)

Morley Building Materials Ltd
Tel: 01675 468 400
www.thermalite.co.uk
(concrete)

Full Blown Metals Ltd
Tel: 015395 30234
www.fullblownmetals.com
(metals)

Forgetec Engineering
Tel: 01594 835 363
(metals)

Zinc Counters
High Street, Markington, Harrogate
North Yorkshire Tel: 01765 677 808
(metals)

Rimex Metals (UK) Ltd
Tel: 020 8804 0633
www.rimexmetals.com
(metals)

Compass Glass and Glazing
Tel: 020 8946 8080
www.compassglass.co.uk
(glass)

Luxcrete Ltd
Tel: 020 8965 7292 www.luxcrete.co.uk
(glass)

Lightscape Projects Ltd
Tel: 020 7231 5323
(glass)

Louis Poulson UK Ltd
Tel: 01372 848 800
(glass)

Sussex Terracotta
Tel: 01424 756 777
www.sussexterracotta.co.uk
(terracotta, ceramic and brick)

Fired Earth Plc
Tel: 01295 812 088 www.firedearth.com
(tiles)

Ibstock Brick Ltd
Tel: 0870 903 4000 www.ibstock.co.uk
(tiles)

RTC Safety Surface Ltd
Tel: 01282 850 141 www.rtcsafety.co.uk
(rubber)

Jaymart Rubber & Plastics Ltd
Tel: 01373 864 926
(astroturf and rubber matting)

Luc D'Hulst
www.lucdhulst.be
(wood)

US

Gardener's Supply Company
Tel: 800 863 1700
www.gardeners.com
(general garden products)

Bear Creek Lumber
PO Box 669, Winthrop
WA 98862 Tel: 800 597 7191
(wood)

High Plains Stone
PO Box 100, Castle Rock
CO 80104 Tel: 303 791 1862
(stone)

The Home Depot
www.HomeDepot.com
(general garden products)

Lowe's Home Improvement Warehouse
www.lowes.com
(general garden products)

AUSTRALIA

Jardinique
Shop 6, Reginald Street, Cremorne
NSW 2090 Tel: 02 9908 7000
(general garden products)

The Parterre Garden
33 Ocean Street, Woollahra
NSW 2025 Tel: 02 9363 5874
(general garden products)

Cotswold Garden Furniture
42 Hotham Parade, Artarmon
NSW\2064 Tel: 02 9906 5417
(furniture)

Porter's Original Paints
Distributed in all states, 895 Bourke Street
Waterloo, NSW 2017 Tel: 02 9698 5322
(garden paints)

NEW ZEALAND

Capital Stone Ltd
Tel: 09443 1031
(marble and granite)

Winstone Glass
Tel: 0800 809 010
(glass)

Auckland Glass
Tel: 09415 8995
(glass)

Firth Paving
Tel: 0800 800 576
(bricks and paving)